STEP BY

Using
dBASE III
on the
Amstrad PC

Using dBASEIII on the Amstrad PC

Nigel Roberts

HEINEMANN
NEW TECH

Heinemann Newtech
An imprint of Heinemann Professional Publishing Ltd
Halley Court, Jordan Hill, Oxford OX2 8EJ

OXFORD LONDON MELBOURNE AUCKLAND SINGAPORE
IBADAN NAIROBI GABORONE KINGSTON

First published 1988
Reprinted 1989

© Nigel Roberts

British Library Cataloguing in Publication Data
Roberts, Nigel
   Step by step guide to using dBASE III on the Amstrad PC.
   1. Amstrad PC microcomputer systems.
   Machine-readable file. dBASE III
   Software packages. dBASE III
   I. Title
   005.75′65

ISBN 0 434 91742 7

Typeset by JCA Typesetting, Ringwood, Hampshire
Printed and bound in Great Britain by
Redwood Burn Limited, Trowbridge, Wiltshire

Contents

PART ONE INTRODUCTION TO DATABASES

1	Planning a database management system	10
2	Introduction to dBASEIII and dBASEIII Plus	13
3	Installing dBASEIII and dBASEIII Plus	15
4	Starting dBASE	20

PART TWO SETTING UP A DATABASE

5	The Assistant	24
6	The menu options	26
7	The dot prompt	30
8	Help	31

PART THREE DATABASE FILES

9	Creating a database file	34
10	Entering records to a database file	41
11	Saving the database file	43
12	Displaying, printing a database file and quitting	44

PART FOUR DATA ENTRY FORMS

13	Creating a data entry form	50
14	Using the modify menu	61
15	Printing and saving the data entry form	62

PART FIVE ADDING, DISPLAYING AND EDITING RECORDS

16	Adding records to a database file	64
17	Displaying records using browse	66
18	Editing records	69

PART SIX PROCESSING RECORDS

19	Locating a record	74
20	Indexing records	80
21	Copying records	86
22	Sorting records	92
23	Counting records	97

PART SEVEN QUERIES

24	Creating a query file	100

Contents

PART EIGHT   REPORTS

25	Creating a report	112
26	Report heading and columns	117
27	Modify an existing report	124
28	Displaying and printing reports	129

PART NINE   LABELS

29	Creating labels	134
30	Label contents	136
31	Modify an existing label	141
32	Displaying and printing labels	142

PART TEN   USING THE DOT PROMPT

33	Commands from the dot prompt	146

PART ELEVEN   COMMANDS

34	Summary of dBASEIII commands	162
35	Extra commands used in dBASEIII Plus	172

PART TWELVE   AN INTEGRATED PROGRAM

36	Main menu	176
37	Customer maintenance menu	178
38	Stock maintenance menu	186
39	Print menu	193

Index   205

PART ONE

Introduction to databases

■ SECTION 1
Planning a database management system

The term **database** refers to a body of stored information, but it is often used as a shorthand form of **Database Management System (DBMS)**. DBMS can be defined as a system that will organize the storage of data in such a way as to facilitate its retrieval for many different types of application.

Most organizations will have some form of database, either a manual (paper based) system or a computerized database system.

A paper-based system can be organized in many ways, i.e. different folders in a filing cabinet, or it could be a collection of cards in a box, sorted into alphabetical order.

There are many disadvantages with a paper-based filing system, some are:

- Records can be lost or replaced in the wrong order by the user.
- They can be very bulky, lots of boxes or cabinets.
- It is very difficult to manipulate, display or analyse the data.
- If there are many records, to retrieve them can be very time consuming.

The above are just a few of the disadvantages of a paper-based filing system.

Any form of filing system should be able to fulfil at least two roles in particular:

- To keep track of what has happened in the past.
- To use the information to assist current activities and also be able to plan future activities.

If we look at these two points it is the second one that lends itself to a computer-based system. When using a paper-based filing system, it cannot compete with a computer database system, when it comes to sorting through large pieces of information, and then showing that information in a useful and meaningful format.

■ SECTION 1
Planning a database management system

A good database management system can process information in various ways, i.e. by displaying on a screen or by printing a report. For example, you could ask for a list of all customers who have placed an order with you in the last five weeks, or all the customers who have not been visited by a member of your sales staff in the last five weeks in any area or town.

It is also possible for many databases to perform calculations, such as being able to total all the amounts owed on all the outstanding invoices, or it is possible to compare the sales in one area with another area. If you were using a card index system, it could not be expected to give an answer immediately, but only after a lengthy search and calculations. But a computerized database system can solve these problems very quickly.

The records in a database file can differ greatly in the information that they contain, but their format is normally fixed and has to be defined in advance by the user before any data can be input into the database file. This process of definition is known as **Creating** and when the format of a database file is created, it is stored on disk awaiting the input of data.

Before you create a format for a database file, the layout of the file should be planned by deciding what items of information are required to be stored on each record on the database file, and therefore what fields will have to be allocated.

It is very important that you work out the size of your records, so that you are able to calculate the number that you will be able to fit into the available storage space. If you use long records they will soon fill a disk, let's look at the following record:

```
Company Name    ************************    (25 characters)
Address         ************************
                ************************
                ************************    (75 characters)
Postcode        ********                    ( 8 characters)
Discount        *****                       ( 5 characters)
Date            ********                    ( 8 characters)
Contact Name    ************************    (25 characters)
                The Total Record Length = 146 Characters
```

■ SECTION 1
Planning a database management system

If we use the previous example, we can calculate the number of records that would say fit onto a floppy disk. The total capacity of a disk is over 360,000 characters and one record will take up 146 characters, therefore 360,000/146 = 2465 complete records can be stored on the disk.

When designing your database record it is important to allow space in each field for most eventualities that may occur, i.e. longer names or addresses.

A computer database system can sort, search for, retrieve and print out data using any field or combination of fields very quickly as compared with a paper-based filing system.

■ SECTION 2
Introduction to dBASE III and dBASE III Plus

dBASEIII was first introduced in 1984 and was designed for the 16–bit microprocessor. The program was written in C and was designed to support menus, which made its use much simpler for the non-programmer.

dBASEIII Plus was then introduced in late 1985. Two of the main differences between dBASEIII and dBASEIII Plus are that the latter has networking capabilities and a far superior menu system, allowing most of the commands and functions to be accessed from it and therefore not having to use the dot prompt as in dBASEIII. These menus are also a very good teaching aid in their own right, because when an Option is selected from the menus, the correct dot command will be shown above the status bar.

Both programs have the following system requirements:

- A minimum of 256k of memory.
- Require MS-DOS or PC-DOS Versions 2.0 or later.
- Twin 360k double sided floppy-disk drives or one 360k floppy-disk drive plus a hard-disk drive.

dBASEIII and dBASEIII Plus both support the following file types with the following extensions:

.dbf	.DBF	—	Database file
.dbt	.DBT	—	Database memo fields file
.fmt	.FMT	—	Format file
.frm	.FRM	—	Report form file
.lbl	.LBL	—	Label form file
.mem	.MEM	—	Memory file
.ndx	.NDX	—	Index file
.prg	.PRG	—	Command or program file
.txt	.TXT	—	Text output file

dBASEIII Plus has the following extra file types that are not available to dBASEIII.

.cat	.CAT	—	Catalog file
.qry	.QRY	—	Query file
.scr	.SCR	—	Screen file
.vue	.VUE	—	View file

SECTION 2
Introduction to dBASE III and dBASE III Plus

A file name can be up to eight characters long and must begin with a letter, it can contain letters, numbers and underscores (_). Embedded blank spaces are not allowed in any file names.

Field names and memory variables can be up to ten characters long and must begin with a letter, it can contain letters, numbers and underscores (_). Embedded blank spaces and any other characters are not allowed.

A character field is able to store up to 254 characters of information.

A memo field in dBASEIII can store up to 4000 characters of information.

A memo field in dBASEIII Plus can store up to 5000 bytes or the capacity of the word processor used.

A numeric field is able to store up to 19 characters of information, and can include decimal points, digits, and the sign values + or −, but the use of commas, etc. is not allowed.

A date field is eight characters long and is set out in the format mm/dd/yy, but can be altered from the American standard to British, dd/mm/yy.

A database file can contain up to two billion characters of information or a maximum of up to one billion records per file. Each record can have up to 4000 characters and up to a maximum of 128 fields. This amount of characters can only be stored if the disk storage space is available.

In a database memo (.DBT) file, up to 512,000 characters may be stored.

A maximum of 10 database files (.DBF) can be open at any one time. (A database file can count as two files if memo fields are used.)

Seven index files can be open in an active database file.

One open format file can be open in an active database file.

The total number of files of all types allowed open is 15.

■ SECTION 3
Installing dBASE III and dBASE III Plus

Floppy-disk system

dBASE can be run from the two system disks as supplied. System Disk #1 is copy protected and System Disk #2 is not. It is therefore advisable to make a backup copy of System Disk #2 and store the original in a safe place. If the copy then becomes damaged in any way, you are able to make another copy, if System Disk #1 becomes damaged in any way you should then return it to Ashton-Tate.

To make a backup copy of System Disk #2:

1 Boot up the system with the DOS system disk in drive A.

2 When the **A>** is shown, type:

   A>DISKCOPY A: B:

3 The following prompt will then be shown:

   Insert source diskette in drive A:

   Insert target diskette in drive B:

   Strike any key when ready

(This message may vary, depending on the DOS that is being used.)

4 Remove the DOS disk from drive A and insert System Disk #2.

5 Insert a blank disk in drive B. This can be a formatted or unformatted disk, as the DISKCOPY command will format a disk while it is copying.

6 When the copying is finished the following message will appear:

   Copy complete

   Copy another (Y/N)?

7 Answer 'n' to the prompt, to end the copying process.

SECTION 3
Installing dBASE III and dBASE III Plus

The System Disk #1, should now have certain system information copied to it from the DOS system disk, to enable you to boot the computer up from System Disk #1:

1 Insert the DOS system disk in drive A and boot up the system.

2 Insert the dBASE System Disk #1 in drive B.

3 Type at the **A>** prompt:

A>SYS B:

4 When completed, the following message will be shown:

System transferred

5 Now type at the **A>** prompt:

A>COPY COMMAND.COM B:

6 When the **A>** prompt reappears, the system transfer will have been completed.

dBASEIII Plus hard-disk system

To install dBASE onto a hard disk your computer must have at least one 360k floppy disk drive to install the program onto the hard disk. To start the installation you will need System Disk #1, System Disk #2 and DOS:

1 Boot up the computer and wait for the prompt **C>**. If the **A>** prompt is showing you can change it to the **C>** prompt by typing **C:** at the **A>** prompt

A>C:

2 Now create a subdirectory to store dBASE in, by typing:

C>MD DBASE

3 Insert System Disk #1 in drive A.

■ SECTION 3
Installing dBASE III and dBASE III Plus

4 Change the current drive to A, by typing:

C>A:

5 At the A> prompt type:

A>INSTALL C:

The screen as shown in Figure 3-2 will describe the installation procedure.

Strike a key and you will be prompted to verify that your hard disk is drive C and that your System Disk #1 is in drive A. If true press enter to continue.

6 You will then be informed that the program can only be installed onto the hard disk a maximum of one time. Type Y to continue.

```
Ashton-Tate
dBASE III PLUS Hard Disk Installation        (2.0.3)

Insert System Disk 1 in drive = A

Hard Disk Drive = C

Confirm that System Disk 1 is in drive = A:
hit RETURN ( ↵ ) to continue
```

Figure 3-1

■ SECTION 3
Installing dBASE III and dBASE III Plus

```
                dBASE III PLUS VERSION 1.1
                   HARD DISK INSTALLATION
    You can copy dBASE III PLUS to your hard disk by following
    these installation instructions. You can also use these
    instructions to install dBASE ADMINISTRATOR.

    If you want to save a previously installed version of dBASE,
    uninstall it using that version's UNINSTAL program.

    If you choose not to save a previous version, install dBASE
    III PLUS Version 1.1 into the same directory. This will
    automatically erase the previous version of dBASE.

    dBASE III PLUS will be installed on drive c:

    Do you want to continue (Y/N)?
```

Figure 3-2

7 The message **dBASEIII Plus copy-protected files now installed** will be shown on the screen. When several files have been copied from your System Disk #1 onto the hard disk, you will be prompted to insert your System Disk #2 into drive A.

8 When several files have been copied from the System Disk #2 onto your hard disk, a message **dBASEIII Plus has been successfully installed** will be shown on the screen.

9 Installation is now complete, and you are now ready to use dBASEIII Plus from the hard disk.

dBASEIII

To install dBASEIII on a hard disk there must be a minimum of two megabytes of available disk space on the hard disk, or you will get the following message:

Target media type incorrect (code 0104).

Now follow the following steps:

■ SECTION 3
Installing dBASE III and dBASE III Plus

1 First set the default drive to A, and then insert System Disk #1 in drive A.

2 Now type:

A>COPY CONFIG.SYS <c:\>

and press RETURN, where <c:\> represents the root directory of the boot drive.

3 Now create the directory where you want the dBASEIII program files copied to be the default directory on the hard disk. This can be done from either drive A or C:

C>CD \DBASE

or

A>CD C:\DBASE

4 Now insert System Disk #1 in drive A and type:

A>INSTALL C:

5 The Hard Disk Installation Screen will be shown, press any key to continue.

6 The following screen will now be shown:

**The maximum dBASEIII install amount is 0001
After this install, 0000 install will be available.
Press RETURN (↵) to continue, Ctrl-Break to abort.**

Press RETURN as prompted.

7 You will be prompted to insert System Disk #2 in drive A and press a key when ready. When finished remove System Disk #2 from drive A.

8 Now check that dBASEIII has been installed correctly, at the **C>** prompt type:

C>DBASE

The dBASEIII copyright notice and dot prompt will be seen.

SECTION 4
Starting dBASE

dBASEIII Plus

To start dBASEIII Plus on a twin disk drive follow the steps shown below:

1 Insert the System Disk #1 into drive A and boot the computer.

2 At the prompt enter the current date and press the RETURN key, and then enter the current time when prompted.

3 At the **A>** prompt type:

   A>DBASE

4 When the License Agreement screen appears, press RETURN to continue.

5 dBASE will then show the following message:

   Insert System Disk 2 and press ENTER...

   at the bottom of the screen, remove Disk #1 and insert System Disk #2 in drive A and press RETURN.

6 The Assistant menu will then be shown, as in Figure 5–1.

To start dBASEIII Plus from a hard disk follow the steps shown below:

1 Boot the computer and then move to the DBASE subdirectory by typing at the **C>** prompt

   C>CD\DBASE

2 When the **C>** prompt is shown again type:

   C>DBASE

3 When the License Agreement screen appears, press RETURN to continue.

■ SECTION 4
Starting dBASE

4 The Assistant menu will then be shown, as in Figure 5–1, and dBASEIII Plus will be ready to use.

dBASEIII

To run dBASEIII follow the same procedures as for dBASEIII Plus, the only main difference will be that the Assistant screen will not be shown, but the copyright notice and the dot prompt will be shown.

PART TWO

Setting up a database

■ SECTION 5
The Assistant

dBASEIII Plus

When dBASEIII Plus is started using the system disk or a hard disk, the Assistant's opening menu will appear at the top of the screen showing the various menu options that are available as shown in Figure 5-1. If the Assistant's opening menu does not appear on the screen, it probably means that your dBASEIII Plus program has not been installed. Refer back to section 3 and follow the instructions on installing dBASEIII Plus.

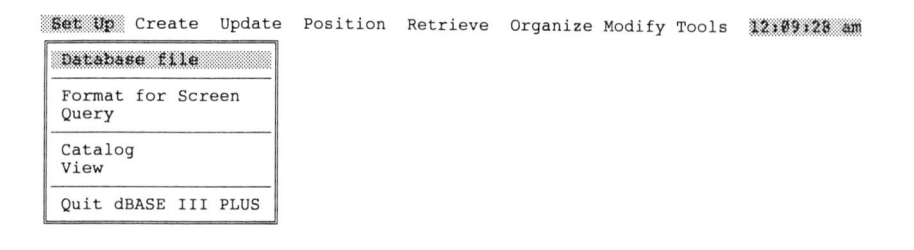

```
Set Up  Create  Update  Position  Retrieve  Organize  Modify  Tools    12:09:28 am
┌─────────────────────┐
│ Database file       │
├─────────────────────┤
│ Format for Screen   │
│ Query               │
│                     │
│ Catalog             │
│ View                │
│                     │
│ Quit dBASE III PLUS │
└─────────────────────┘




ASSIST          |<A:>|                          |Opt: 1/6|
```

Figure 5-1

dBASEIII

When dBASEIII is loaded the Assistant is not automatically shown on the screen, all that will be seen is the dot prompt (Figure 7-2), when the dot prompt is displayed enter the command ASSIST. The Assistant key/function screen will be displayed as shown in Figure 5-2

SECTION 5
The Assistant

A:\>

```
                         The dBASE III
                           Assistant
       Assist uses menus to bring you the power of dBASE III
```

KEY	FUNCTION
Esc	Exit from current operation.
Up arrow (↑)	Move to previous menu.
Down arrow (↓)	Move to next menu.
Left arrow (←)	Move one item to the left.
Right arrow (→)	Move one item to the right.
Home	Go to first menu.
End	Go to right most item.
Option Letter	Executes option (Unless otherwise noted option letter is first letter of option.)

```
         PRESS ↵ (or ENTER) TO CONTINUE, ESC to EXIT ASSIST:
```

Figure 5-2

■ SECTION 6
The menu options

dBASEIII Plus

To open other menus press the right arrow key (→) to move along the menu bar, to save time you may press the left arrow key (←) when the screen looks as Figure 5–1 to move straight to the Tools menu. It is also possible to open a menu on the menu bar by typing the first letter of its name, if you pressed M, the Modify menu would open. In Figure 6–1 the menu bar plus all the submenus are shown.

```
Set Up                  Create              Update

Database File           Database File       Append
Format for Screen       Format              Edit
Query                   View                Display
Catalog                 Query               Browse
View                    Report              Replace
Quit dBASE III Plus     Label               Delete
                                            Recall
                                            Pack


Position                Retrieve            Organize

Seek                    List                Index
Locate                  Display             Sort
Continue                Report              Copy
Skip                    Label
Goto Record             Sum
                        Average
                        Count


Modify                  Tools

Database File           Set Drive
Format                  Copy File
View                    Directory
Query                   Rename
Report                  Erase
Label                   List Structure
                        Import
                        Export
```

Figure 6–1

From many of these submenus there are further submenus, for example, if you picked the RETRIEVE menu on the menu bar and then chose List the following submenu of list would be shown next to it:

■ SECTION 6
The menu options

```
Set Up  Create  Update  Position  Retrieve  Organize Modify Tools   12:13:49 am
                                  ┌─────────┬──────────────────────────┐
                                  │ List    │ Execute the command      │
                                  │ Display │ Specify scope            │
                                  │ Report  │ Construct a field list   │
                                  │ Label   │ Build a search condition │
                                  │─────────│ Build a scope condition  │
                                  │ Sum     └──────────────────────────┘
                                  │ Average
                                  │ Count
                                  └─────────

Command: LIST
ASSIST              <B:> CUSTOMER              Rec: 1/11
```

Figure 6–2

■ SECTION 6
The menu options

When using submenus you will find that there are further submenus in many cases.

dBASEIII

To access the first Assistant menu from the Assistant key/function screen press the RETURN (↵) key, the screen will look as follows:

```
                        dBASE III Assistant                    READY
Set Up      Modify      Position       Retrieve    Organize    Utilities
Use or Create a database and Create Reports or Label Forms.
```

```
                        SET UP ENVIRONMENT
The  SET UP menu allows you to establish the active database file either
by  creating a new one or selecting an existing one.  It also lets  you
create  label and report layouts.  Other menu options are inactive until
an active database is available.

Use       Set Drive     Create       Create Label    Create Report
```

```
No database is in use.  Press to select SET UP to define a USE file.
   Left:   Right:   Next:   (or ENTER)    Help: F1
```

Figure 6–3

■ SECTION 6
The menu options

As in dBASEIII Plus there are various submenus and these can be accessed by pressing the arrow (← →) keys. In Figure 6–4 the menu bar and all the submenus are shown.

```
Set Up           Modify         Position        Retrieve       Organize

Use              Append         Find            Display        Index
Set Drive        Browse         Locate          Sum            Sort
Create           Edit           Continue        Average        Copy
Create Label     Delete         Skip            Count          Pack
Create Report    Recall         Go              Label
                 Replace        Modify          Report
                 Position       Retrieve        Position
Utilities

Set drive
Copy file
Dir
Rename
Erase
Modify structure
```

Figure 6–4

SECTION 7
The dot prompt

To enter the dot prompt mode when using the Assistant press the Esc (escape) key; the number of times that you have to press this key will depend upon which submenu you are in, keep on pressing the Esc key until you return to the main menu then press once more to leave the Assistant and enter the Dot Prompt Mode. The screen will now be cleared except for the status line and the dot prompt which can be seen directly above the status line, this can be seen in Figure 7–1. When in the dot prompt mode you are able to enter dBASEIII commands, for example you can show all the records in the current database by entering the command List at the dot prompt.

| Command Line | <B:>CUSTOMER | Rec: 1/11 | | |

Figure 7–1

■ SECTION 8
Help

dBASEIII has a built-in Help system. When using dBASEIII you can obtain information about the function of a command or menu option by pressing the Help function key **'F1'**. When this key is pressed a Help screen is displayed, see Figure 8–1. After reading the message you can return to the screen that you were in before by pressing any key.

```
                          dBASE III Assistant                      READY
░░░░░░░    Modify         Position     Retrieve    Organize      Utilities
Use or Create a database and Create Reports or Label Forms.
┌─────────────────────────────────────────────────────────────────────────┐
│                    ASSIST COMMAND NAVIGATION GUIDE                      │
│  Set up        Modify      Position    Retrieve   Organize   Utilities  │
│                                                                         │
│  Use           Append      Find        Display    Index      Set Drive  │
│  Set Drive     Browse      Locate      Sum        Sort       Copy File  │
│  Create        Edit        Continue    Average    Copy       Dir        │
│  Create Label  Delete      Skip        Count      Pack       Rename     │
│  Create Report Recall      Go          Label                 Erase      │
│                Replace     Modify      Report                Modify Stru.│
│                Position    Retrieve    Position                         │
└─────────────────────────────────────────────────────────────────────────┘

░░░░░░░░░░░░░░░░░░░░░░░░░░░░░░░░░░░░░░░░░░░░░░░░░░░░░░░░░░░░░░░░░
```

Figure 8–1

When you are in the dot prompt mode and you have entered a command and it is wrong, such as a misspelling, i.e. LAST as LIST, dBASEIII will ask;

Do you want some help?(Y/N)

If you typed 'Y', the Help screen would be displayed for the word List, see Figure 8–2. To go to the Help screen menu, press F10 and the HELP MAIN MENU will be displayed.

■ SECTION 8
Help

LIST

Syntax : LIST [<scope>] [<expression list>] [FOR <condition>]
                [WHILE <condition>] [OFF] [TO PRINT]

Description : Displays the contents of a database file.
              Used alone, it displays all records. Use the scope and
              FOR/WHILE clauses to list selectively. The expression
              list can be included to select fields or a combination
              of fields, such as Cost * Rate. OFF suppresses the record
              numbers.

```
HELP              |<C:>|                              |                |   Caps
 Previous screen - PgUp. Previous menu - F10. Exit with Esc or enter a command.
                    ENTER >
```

Figure 8–2

PART THREE

Database files

■ SECTION 9
Creating a database file

To create a database file, the command to use is CREATE, this can be used by choosing the CREATE option from the Assistant menu or by entering the command CREATE (filename) at the dot prompt.

In this section we will create a database file named CUSTOMER, in which we will keep a record of customers' names and addresses plus other relevant information.

dBASEIII Plus

Press the right arrow key and move the highlighted block to create the file (see Figure 5–1). When create is selected the first item of the submenu, Database File is highlighted, this is indicating that the option highlighted is the current option, now press the RETURN key, you will then be prompted to select a disk drive on which to store your database file. Drive A will be shown highlighted, use the arrow key to move the highlight to specify Drive B (see Figure 9–1), press RETURN and you will then be prompted to enter the name of the database file, enter the name CUSTOMER (see Figure 9–2).

```
Set Up  Create  Update  Position  Retrieve  Organize Modify Tools    12:16:16 am
        ┌──────────────┐
        │Database file │ ┌────┐
        │Format        │ │ A: │
        │View          │ │ B: │
        │Query         │ │ C: │
        │Report        │ │ D: │
        │Label         │ │ E: │
        └──────────────┘ └────┘




Command: CREATE
ASSIST          <B:>CUSTOMER              Rec: 1/11
```

Figure 9–1

■ SECTION 9
Creating a database file

When the file name has been entered, if you then press the Esc key, a message will then appear in the message window:

Are you sure you want to abandon operation? (Y/N)

If 'Y' is pressed, the create operation will be aborted and you will be returned to the Assistant menu. If 'N' is pressed, you are able to continue creating the file.

```
Set Up  Create  Update  Position  Retrieve  Organize Modify Tools   12:17:33 am
        ┌─────────────────┐
        │ Database file   │
        │ Format          │
        │ View            │
        │ Query           │
        │ Report          │
        │ Label           │
        └─────────────────┘
                ┌──────────────────────────────────────────────┐
                │ Enter the name of the file: CUSTOMER         │
                └──────────────────────────────────────────────┘




Command: CREATE B:
ASSIST         |<B:>|CUSTOMER              |Rec: 1/11       |        |    Caps
```

Figure 9–2

35

■ SECTION 9
Creating a database file

To continue entering the file name press RETURN and you will see a blank table for creating the structure of the file, the screen will look as follows:

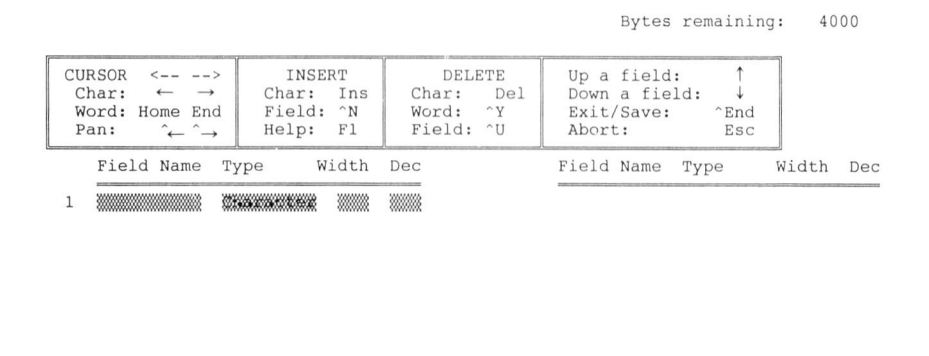

```
                                              Bytes remaining:   4000

 CURSOR   <-- -->    INSERT           DELETE       Up a field:    ↑
 Char:     ←   →     Char:   Ins      Char:  Del   Down a field:  ↓
 Word: Home End      Field:  ^N       Word:  ^Y    Exit/Save:     ^End
 Pan:      ^← ^→     Help:   F1       Field: ^U    Abort:         Esc

     Field Name   Type    Width   Dec         Field Name   Type    Width   Dec
  1  ▓▓▓▓▓▓▓▓▓▓   ▓▓▓▓▓▓▓ ▓▓▓▓    ▓▓▓▓
```

Figure 9-3

Now let's create our first database file – **CUSTOMER.DBF**

On line one against Field Name enter: **CUST_NO** and press RETURN.

The cursor will then move to the field Type, Figure 9-4 shows the various field types and describes them, you are able to change the field type by pressing the spacebar. Select **character** and press RETURN (it is also possible to select a field type, by entering the first letter of the field name: c for character, n for numeric, d for date, l for logical and m for memo). Enter **4** for width, press RETURN and the cursor will automatically move to the start of field two. Now enter the rest of the fields as shown in Table One below:

36

SECTION 9
Creating a database file

Field Name	Type	Width	Dec
CUST_NAME	CHARACTER	36	
ADD_1	CHARACTER	25	
ADD_2	CHARACTER	25	
ADD_3	CHARACTER	25	
POSTCODE	CHARACTER	8	
DISCOUNT	NUMERIC	4	2
DATE	DATE	8	
TEL_NO	CHARACTER	12	
CONTACT	CHARACTER	35	

Table One

On the DISCOUNT field, after the Width of 4 has been entered the cursor will not automatically move to the next field but to the DEC field, if there is no entry just press RETURN.

TYPE	DESCRIPTION
Character	— This may include letters, numbers and punctuation symbols, numbers used in this type will not be calculated, therefore use for telephone numbers, etc.
Numeric	— Numbers can be calculated and can include a decimal point, a leading plus (+) or minus (−) sign.
Date	— Sets the width to eight characters automatically and the date is entered in the format 12/30/87 (MM/DD/YY).
Logical	— This is a true/false or a yes/no response (for example: the answer to the question "Paid/Not Paid?").
Memo	— This will allow text entry of up to 5000 characters (dBASE III Plus) or 4000 characters (dBASE III). It may be created with a word processor or a text editor, it will be stored as a separate file on disk, and it will also give a field length of 10 automatically.

Figure 9–4

■ SECTION 9
Creating a database file

When all the above fields have been entered, the file should look as follows:

```
                                              Bytes remaining:    3817

    CURSOR    <-- -->     INSERT           DELETE         Up a field:    ↑
      Char:    ←  →       Char:   Ins      Char:    Del   Down a field:  ↓
      Word: Home End      Field:  ^N       Word:    ^Y    Exit/Save:     ^End
      Pan:     ^← ^→      Help:   F1       Field:   ^U    Abort:         Esc

        Field Name    Type      Width  Dec              Field Name   Type        Width  Dec
    1   CUST_NO       Character    4                9   TEL_NO       Character     12
    2   CUST_NAME     Character   36               10
    3   ADD_1         Character   25
    4   ADD_2         Character   25
    5   ADD_3         Character   25
    6   POSTCODE      Character    8
    7   DISCOUNT      Numeric      4    2
    8   DATE          Date         8
```

Figure 9-5

dBASEIII

At the dot prompt type **ASSIST** and press the RETURN key, press the down arrow key and then select the **Set Up** menu and press the down arrow key. Move the highlighted bar to the **Set Drive** submenu and press the down arrow key, the screen should now look as in Figure 9-6. Select **B** and press the RETURN key.

■ SECTION 9
Creating a database file

```
                        Set Up Environment                    READY
Use        Set Drive      Create       Create Label    Create Report
Select a database to be processed.
```

```
                              USE
USE allows you to select the active or working database file from
existing database files and optionally, an index file. Subsequent
commands will operate on this database file until another one is
selected.  You may designate the disk drive for both the database file
and the index file.  Use the CREATE menu option if a new database file is
needed.

         Command Format: USE <file name> [INDEX <index file list>]
                         [ALIAS <alias name>]
```

`Command: Use`

Figure 9-6

Now move the highlighted bar to the **Create** menu and press the down arrow key, dBASEIII will then prompt you for the name of the file, enter CUSTOMER and press the RETURN key, see Figure 9–7.

Now let's create a database file named **CUSTOMER.DBF**, enter the information in the database fields as in the dBASEIII Plus section and then save by pressing the **Ctrl–End** keys. dBASEIII will then prompt:

Input data records now?(Y/N)

39

■ SECTION 9
Creating a database file

```
                           Set Up Environment
Use          Set Drive     Create          Create Label          Create Report
Create a database.  (C - Option letter)
```

```
A file name can consist of from 1 to 8 letters or digits.  A disk drive
letter (A,B..) and a colon can precede the file name.  Otherwise, current
disk drive is used.     Enter the name of the file: CUSTOMER
Command: Create
```

Figure 9-7

Answer 'Y' and the screen will now look as in Figure 10-1.

■ SECTION 10
Entering records to a database file

Before you are able to enter records to your database it must be saved first, to do this:

Press Ctrl–End

dBASE will then prompt:

Press ENTER to confirm. Any other key to resume

A message **Please Wait** ... will appear and when the database file structure has been saved dBASE will ask:

Input data records now? (Y/N)

Enter 'Y' to enter data, a template screen will now appear.

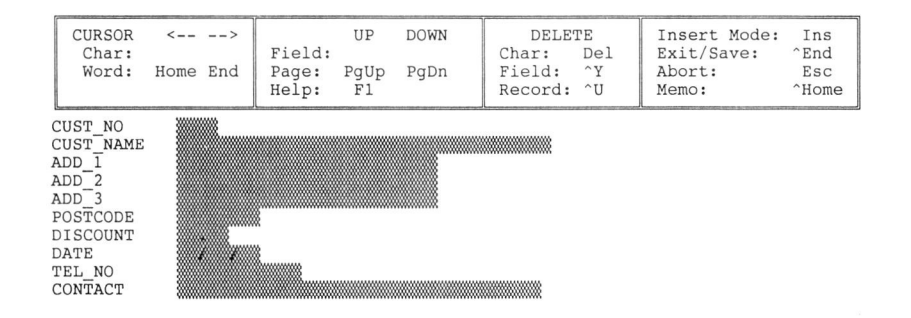

```
CURSOR    <-- -->         UP    DOWN      DELETE         Insert Mode:   Ins
Char:            Field:                   Char:    Del   Exit/Save:    ^End
Word:   Home End Page:  PgUp  PgDn        Field:   ^Y    Abort:         Esc
                 Help:    F1               Record:  ^U    Memo:        ^Home
```

```
CUST_NO
CUST_NAME
ADD_1
ADD_2
ADD_3
POSTCODE
DISCOUNT
DATE
TEL_NO
CONTACT
```

Figure 10–1

Now enter the following information to complete the customer records:

41

■ SECTION 10
Entering records to a database file

C001	against CUST_NO, you will notice that the cursor has moved to the next field automatically, this will happen when there is no space left in the field.
JONES A.J.	against CUST_NAME and press RETURN
89 CITY ROAD	against ADD_1 and press RETURN
SWANSEA	against ADD_2 and press RETURN
WEST GLAMORGAN	against ADD_3 and press RETURN
SA1 8RG	against POSTCODE and press RETURN
10	against DISCOUNT and press RETURN
123087	against DATE
0792 496421	against TEL_NO and press RETURN
ALUN WILLIAMS	against CONTACT and press RETURN

After the last entry has been made and the RETURN key pressed a new blank screen will be shown for the entry of the next record, you can now enter the following records to complete the database file:

Field	Record 2	Record 3	Record 4
CUST_NO	C002	C003	C004
CUST_NAME	LUBRICAL LTD	COMCOL LTD	OKONI UK. LTD
ADD_1	ELTHAM WORKS	AIMTREE ROAD	OKONI HOUSE
ADD_2	PRODHOE	DOUGLAS	KINGSTON UPON THAMES
ADD_3	NORTHUMBERLAND	ISLE OF MAN	SURREY
POSTCODE	NE40 9JP	IM56 4SD	KT41 9PS
DISCOUNT	7.5	4.5	8.5
DATE	102086	091286	080885
TEL_NO	0721 433346	0659 597821	01 541 49621
CONTACT	MARTIN PETERS	ROBERT JAMES	SALLY THOMPSON

Field	Record 5	Record 6	Record 7
CUST_NO	C005	C006	C007
CUST_NAME	SAA LTD	MANNS LIMITED	XYZ SYSTEMS LTD
ADD_1	RAVEN STREET	MOOR LANE	12 RAM ROAD
ADD_2	KEELE	WOKINGHAM	TOTNES
ADD_3	STAFFORDSHIRE	BERKSHIRE	DEVON
POSTCODE	SA42 2JA	RG13 9QR	TQ4 2ST
DISCOUNT	5	4.5	2.5
DATE	042986	020287	011586
TEL_NO	0782 64921	0734 7482	080426 492
CONTACT	BRIAN MORGAN	JOHN WALTERS	MARY CAVE

Field	Record 8
CUST_NO	C008
CUST_NAME	AMAD LTD
ADD_1	78 WILES ROAD
ADD_2	FELTHAM
ADD_3	MIDDX.
POSTCODE	TW11 3DE
DISCOUNT	10
DATE	040986
TEL_NO	01 751 4311
CONTACT	ANDREW ROBERTS

■ SECTION 11
Saving the database file

If you want to re-check your entries, simply press either Pg Up (Page up) or Pg Dn (Page down) to move through the records. When you are satisfied that they are correct press Ctrl-End to save the last record that was entered and to exit creating records. After saving, the Assistant menu will be shown again.

■ SECTION 12
Displaying, printing a database file and quitting

Now that the records have been entered, we will see how to list some of the fields on the records, first move the highlighted bar to Retrieve, select List and then press RETURN, the List submenu will then appear.

Move the highlighted bar to 'Construct a Field List' and press RETURN. A submenu of the fields in the file CUSTOMER.DBF will appear in a box on the left of the screen, as shown in Figure 12–1.

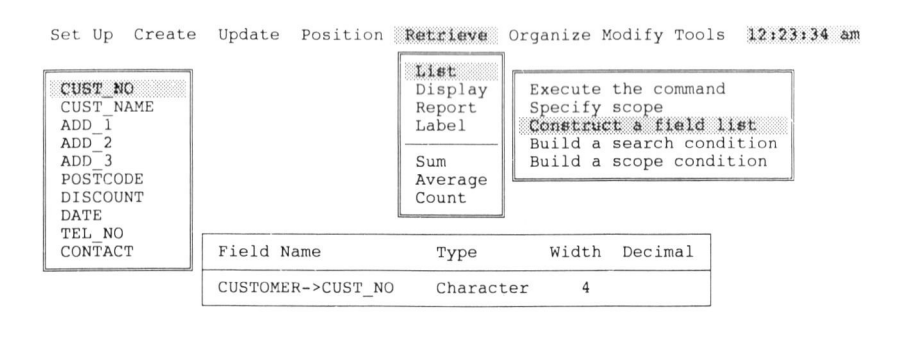

```
Set Up   Create   Update   Position   Retrieve   Organize Modify Tools   12:23:34 am

 CUST_NO                      List
 CUST_NAME                    Display       Execute the command
 ADD_1                        Report        Specify scope
 ADD_2                        Label         Construct a field list
 ADD_3                        ──────        Build a search condition
 POSTCODE                     Sum           Build a scope condition
 DISCOUNT                     Average
 DATE                         Count
 TEL_NO
 CONTACT          Field Name              Type         Width   Decimal

                  CUSTOMER->CUST_NO       Character      4


Command: LIST
ASSIST           |<B:>|CUSTOMER            |Rec: 1/11                   | Caps
```

Figure 12–1

Now select the fields that we want to list. The highlighted bar is positioned on CUST_NO, press RETURN and it moves to the next field CUST_NAME, press RETURN and then move the highlighted bar with the arrow (↓) key down to DISCOUNT, press RETURN and move again to TEL_NO and press RETURN. We have now selected the fields that we require to be listed.

To leave the menu press the right arrow (→) key once to return to the first submenu, move the highlighted bar to **Execute the command** and press RETURN. dBASEIII Plus will then prompt you on the screen with:

Direct the output to the printer?[Y/N]

■ SECTION 12
Displaying, printing a database file and quitting

If you press RETURN the default 'N' will be selected and the records will be displayed on the screen.

```
Record#   CUST_NO   CUST_NAME              DISCOUNT   TEL_NO
     1    C001      JONES A.J.               10.00    0792 496421
     2    C002      LUBRICAL LTD              7.50    0721 433346
     3    C003      COMCOL LTD                4.50    0659 597821
     4    C004      OKONI UK. LTD             8.50    01 541 49621
     5    C005      SAA LTD                   5.00    0782 64921
     6    C006      MANNS LIMITED             4.50    0734 7482
     7    C007      XYZ SYSTEMS LIMITED       2.50    080426 492
     8    C008      AMAD LTD                 10.00    01 751 4311
```

Figure 12-2

If 'Y' was pressed the output would have been to the printer.

dBASEIII

Press the up arrow key to exit the **Set Up Environment** menu and return to the **dBASEIII Assistant** menu. Move the highlighted bar to the **Retrieve** menu and press the down arrow key. Select **Display** and press the down arrow key then press RETURN twice, a submenu of the fields in the database file CUSTOMER.DBF will be seen as in Figure 12-3. We will now construct the list that we require, move the highlighted bar to the CUST_NAME field and press the RETURN key and then select the following fields:

ADD_3

DISCOUNT

pressing the RETURN key each time. Now press the right arrow key to exit the submenu.

SECTION 12
Displaying, printing a database file and quitting

```
                         Retrieve and Present Information
 Display     Sum     Average     Count     Label     Report     Position
Select Field names - Position using  /  ARROW KEYS  -  Select using ENTER
```

```
                         Field Name    Field Type    Width    Dec. #
                         CUST_NO       Character       4
                         CUST_NAME     Character      36
                         ADD_1         Character      25
                         ADD_2         Character      25
                         ADD_3         Character      25
                         POSTCODE      Character       8
                         DISCOUNT      Numeric         5        2
                         DATE          Date            8
                         TEL_NO        Character      12
                         CONTACT       Character      35
```

Command: Display

Figure 12–3

■ SECTION 12
Displaying, printing a database file and quitting

You will now be shown a **Scope** submenu, move the highlighted bar to **ALL** and press the RETURN key, then the **Select conditional statement** screen will be displayed, at this time we will not use this screen. Press the right arrow key and dBASEIII will display all the records on the screen as shown below:

```
                        Retrieve and Present Information
Display      Sum      Average      Count      Label      Report      Position
```
```
Select scope element
```
```
              Process current record (no scope specified)
   NEXT       For the NEXT N records
   ALL        Process ALL the database records
   RECORD     Process one specified record
```

Command: Display

Figure 12-4

47

PART FOUR

Data entry forms

■ SECTION 13
Creating a data entry form

dBASEIII Plus

The way information is input into the database file on the screen can be made to look like an actual form that one would fill in. To do this we will need to create a data entry form and this can be done by using a feature in dBASEIII Plus called Screen Painter, using this you can design your own forms on the screen from our existing database file CUSTOMER.

To create our data entry form ensure that you are in the Assistant menu, then select the Create menu, move the highlighted bar to Format and press RETURN. Select Drive B, and dBASEIII Plus will then prompt you to:

Enter the name of the file

Type CUSTSCR and then press RETURN. The Screen Painter menu bar will then appear as shown below:

```
Set Up          Modify          Options          Exit   12:25:49 am
┌─────────────────────────┐
│ Select Database File    │
│ Create New Database File│
├─────────────────────────┤
│ Load Fields             │
└─────────────────────────┘




CREATE SCREEN   |<B:>|B:CUSTSCR.SCR          |Opt: 1/3                        Caps
```

Figure 13–1

50

■ SECTION 13
Creating a data entry form

Let's look at what the menu headings will do:

Set Up — This will select a database file and then put fields from the file into the data entry form.

Modify — This will add a field to a data entry form or will change an existing field. If an existing database file is being used, any changes will also be made to the database file.

Options — This can create a text file image of the form; it will also generate lines or boxes.

Exit — This will save or abandon any changes that have been made to the data entry form.

The Set Up menu will now be open, make sure that the highlighted bar is on **Select Database File** and then press RETURN, a file submenu will be shown, select the file CUSTOMER.DBF and then move the highlighted bar from **Select Database File** to **Load Fields**, press RETURN. A Field submenu will then be shown of the database file CUSTOMER.DBF, see Figure 13–2.

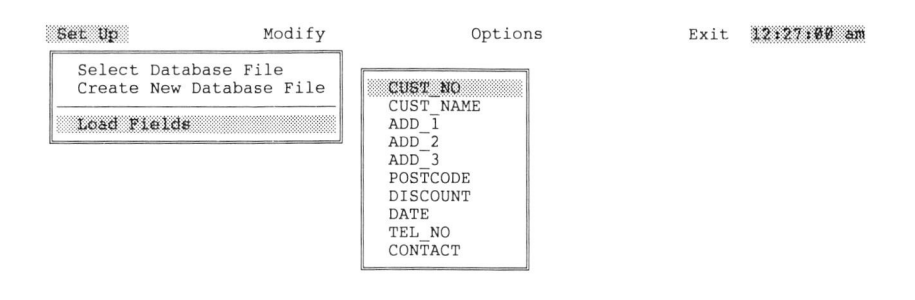

```
Set Up          Modify              Options              Exit    12:27:00 am
┌─────────────────────────┐
│ Select Database File    │
│ Create New Database File│   ┌──────────────┐
│                         │   │ CUST_NO      │
│ Load Fields             │   │ CUST_NAME    │
└─────────────────────────┘   │ ADD_1        │
                              │ ADD_2        │
                              │ ADD_3        │
                              │ POSTCODE     │
                              │ DISCOUNT     │
                              │ DATE         │
                              │ TEL_NO       │
                              │ CONTACT      │
                              └──────────────┘
```

CREATE SCREEN |<B:>|B:CUSTSCR.SCR |Opt: 1/10 | | Caps

Figure 13–2

51

■ SECTION 13
Creating a data entry form

To make our data entry form we will use all the fields in our file, therefore with the highlighted bar in CUST_NO press RETURN, then press the down arrow (↓) key. Press RETURN against each of the fields, after the return key has been pressed the symbol ▶ will appear by each field name.

N.B. If you decide that you do not require a field in the data entry form, just press RETURN again when the highlighted bar is on that field.

When all the fields are marked press the **F10** key, the screen will clear and the Blackboard Screen will be shown as below:

```
Set Up              Modify          Options              Exit   12:30:18 am
CUST_NO      XXXX
CUST_NAME    XXXXXXXXXXXXXXXXXXXXXXXXXXXXXX
ADD_1        XXXXXXXXXXXXXXXXXXXXXX
ADD_2        XXXXXXXXXXXXXXXXXXXXXX
ADD_3        XXXXXXXXXXXXXXXXXXXXXX
POSTCODE     XXXXXXXX
DISCOUNT     99.99
DATE         99/99/99
TEL_NO       XXXXXXXXXXX
CONTACT      XXXXXXXXXXXXXXXXXXXXXXXXXXXXXXXX




CREATE SCREEN   |<B:>|B:CUSTSCR.SCR       |Pg 01 Row 00 Col 00|       | Caps
```

Figure 13-3

52

■ SECTION 13
Creating a data entry form

Now that we are in the Blackboard Screen, we will create our data entry form. Certain keys or combinations of keys can be used when using the Blackboard Screen, these are:

Key	Description
Ins or Ctrl-V	These keys will switch between the Insert and Overwrite modes.
Ctrl-N	This will insert a blank line and shift downward any lines on or below the cursor.
Ctrl-C or PgDn	These keys will scroll the screen forward 20 lines.
Ctrl-R or PgUp	These keys will scroll the screen back by 20 lines.
↑ ↓ ← →	These keys will move the cursor one position in the direction of the indicated arrow key.
Ctrl-A or Home	These keys will move the cursor to the start of the current word or to the start of the previous word.
Ctrl-B or Ctrl-→	These keys will move the cursor to the end of the current line.
Ctrl-F or End	These keys will move the cursor to the start of the next word.
Ctrl-M or ←	These keys will move the cursor to the beginning of the next line. In Insert mode they will insert a blank line. When the cursor is positioned on a field, it will allow you to drag a field to the desired position. When the cursor is positioned on the outline of a box, they will allow the size of the box to be altered.
Ctrl-Z or Ctrl-←	These keys will move the cursor to the beginning of a line.
Ctrl-G or Del	These will delete characters at the current cursor position, if the cursor is positioned on a field it will decrease the width of the field on the form.
Backspace	This will delete characters from the left of the current cursor position.
Ctrl-T	This key will delete all the characters from the current cursor position to the start of the next word.
Ctrl-Y	This will delete the current line.
Ctrl-U	This key will delete the field or box at the current cursor.

Let's now create our data entry form, first place the cursor on **CUST_NO**, ensuring that you are in the Insert mode, if not press the Ins key. Now press RETURN, we now have a blank line above the CUST_NO line.

■ SECTION 13
Creating a data entry form

Move the cursor to Row 01, Col 53 and Type 'Customer Number :', then move the cursor back to the CUST_NO field (XXXX) and press the RETURN key, now move the cursor again using the right arrow key and place it at Row 01, Col 72 and press RETURN. The CUST_NO field will automatically be moved to the new position as shown in Figure 13–4.

```
Set Up            Modify              Options               Exit   12:33:14 am
CUST_NO
CUST_NAME   XXXXXXXXXXXXXXXXXXXXXXXXXXXXXX       Customer Number :  XXXX
ADD_1       XXXXXXXXXXXXXXXXXXXXXXX
ADD_2       XXXXXXXXXXXXXXXXXXXXXXX
ADD_3       XXXXXXXXXXXXXXXXXXXXXXX
POSTCODE    XXXXXXXX
DISCOUNT    99.99
DATE        99/99/99
TEL_NO      XXXXXXXXXXX
CONTACT     XXXXXXXXXXXXXXXXXXXXXXXXXXXXXXXX


CREATE SCREEN   [<B:>[B:CUSTSCR.SCR         [Pg 01 Row 01 Col 72]
```

Figure 13–4

Delete CUST_NO using the Del key.

Now move the other fields and add in the new descriptions as shown in Figure 13–5.
The cursor positions are as follows:

Customer Name	—	Row 04 — Col 12
Address	—	Row 06 — Col 12
Postcode	—	Row 10 — Col 12
Telephone	—	Row 12 — Col 12
Date Account Opened	—	Row 16 — Col 05
Discount	—	Row 16 — Col 50
Contact Name	—	Row 19 — Col 17

54

■ SECTION 13
Creating a data entry form

```
Set Up           Modify              Options              Exit   12:42:23 am
                                                Customer Number  :  XXXX

           Customer Name  :  XXXXXXXXXXXXXXXXXXXXXXXXXXXXXXXXXX
           Address        :  XXXXXXXXXXXXXXXXXXXXXXXXX
                          :  XXXXXXXXXXXXXXXXXXXXXXXXX
                          :  XXXXXXXXXXXXXXXXXXXXXXXXX
           Postcode       :  XXXXXXXX
           Telephone      :  XXXXXXXXXXXX

      Date Account Opened :  99/99/99         Discount  :  99.99

                  Contact Name  :  XXXXXXXXXXXXXXXXXXXXXXXXXXXXXXXXXX
CREATE SCREEN    [<B:>[B:CUSTSCR.SCR          [Pg 01 Row 01 Col 00[Ins
```

Figure 13–5

When all the above has been completed we will place a title on the same line as our Customer number, to do this move the cursor to Row 01, Col 05 and Type 'CUSTOMER RECORD CARD'.

To finish the record card off we will add a few boxes and a dividing line, to do this press **F10** and the Screen Painter Menu bar will appear, now open the Options menu and select:

Draw a window or line – Double bar. (See Figure 13–6)

and then press RETURN, the screen will then show your form again.

55

■ SECTION 13
Creating a data entry form

```
Set Up          Modify          Options           Exit   12:43:47 am
                                ┌─────────────────────────┐
                                │ Generate text file image│
                                ├─────────────────────────┤
                                │ Draw a window or line   │
                                │ Single bar              │
                                │ Double bar              │
                                └─────────────────────────┘
```

```
CREATE SCREEN    |<B:>|B:CUSTSCR.SCR         |Opt: 1/3           |Ins  |
```

Figure 13–6

To draw our first box, move the cursor to Row 00, Col 00 and press RETURN then move the cursor to Row 02, Col 79 and press RETURN again. A double-lined box will be drawn around the title and Customer Number.

Press **F10** again and repeat the selection procedure from the Option menu.

Move the cursor to Row 14, Col 00 and press RETURN, then move the cursor to Row 14, Col 79, press RETURN. A straight double line across the page will be shown.

Press **F10** again and repeat.

Move the cursor to Row 18, Col 00, press RETURN, then move the cursor to Row 20, Col 79 and press RETURN. We now have a double lined box around the Contact Name.

■ SECTION 13
Creating a data entry form

Check the Figure below to ensure that your form is the same:

```
Set Up            Modify              Options              Exit    12:49:29 am
   CUSTOMER RECORD CARD                          Customer Number : XXXX

           Customer Name : XXXXXXXXXXXXXXXXXXXXXXXXXXXXXXXXXXX
           Address       : XXXXXXXXXXXXXXXXXXXXXXX
                         : XXXXXXXXXXXXXXXXXXXXXXX
                         : XXXXXXXXXXXXXXXXXXXXXXX
           Postcode      : XXXXXXXX
           Telephone     : XXXXXXXXXXXX

     Date Account Opened : 99/99/99        Discount : 99.99

                 Contact Name : XXXXXXXXXXXXXXXXXXXXXXXXXXXXXXXXXXX
CREATE SCREEN   |<B:>|B:CUSTSCR.SCR         |Pg 01 Row 20 Col 79|Ins    |
```

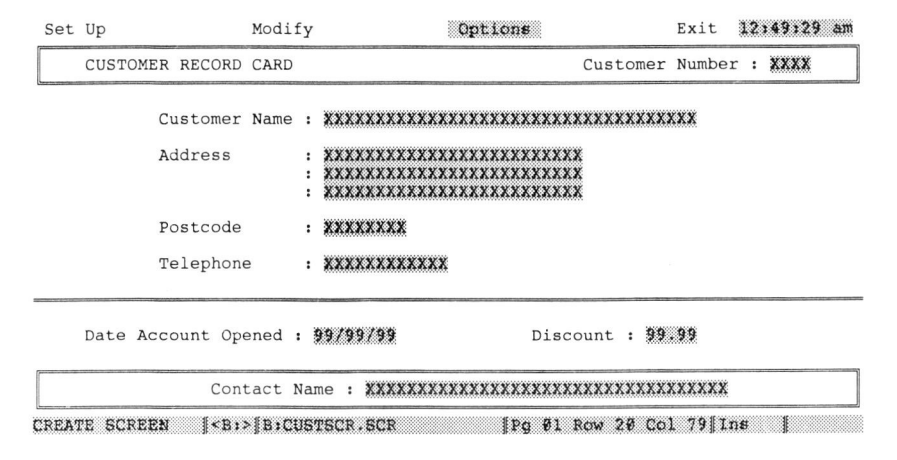

Figure 13–7

dBASEIII

In dBASEIII there is no Screen Painter or Blackboard as in dBASE III Plus. A form can be created in dBASEIII by using the @, **GET, SAY and READ** commands.

To be able to create the form we must firstly exit from the **dBASE III Assistant**, press the up arrow key until you reach the **Assistant key/function** screen, see Figure 6–3, now press the **Esc** key to exit **Assist**.

You now should have the dot prompt of dBASEIII showing. We will now create our form by writing a small and simple program and we will use the following commands:

  @
  SAY
  GET
  READ

Let's look at the various commands above in a little bit more detail:

57

■ SECTION 13
Creating a data entry form

@ Command
This command tells dBASEIII, where on the screen to position the cursor prior to printing. The format for the @ command is as follows

@ ROW,COLUMN
The screen is divided into rows and columns with the upper left corner of the screen being row 0, column 0 and the lower left corner being row, 23 column 0. The screen is 24 rows by 80 columns wide.

SAY Command
This tells dBASEIII what to print at the cursor position as defined by the @ command, look at the following example:

@ 12,29 SAY "CUSTOMER RECORD NUMBER"
Type this in and press the RETURN key and the words **CUSTOMER RECORD NUMBER** will be printed near to the centre of the screen.

GET Command
This command is used with the READ command to accept field and memory variable data from the screen. The format is:

GET field name

READ Command
This command is used with the **@**, **SAY** and **GET** commands to read in field and memory variable data from the screen.

Now let's start creating our form, to do this you can use the **MODIFY** command editor to create our format file. dBASEIII will automatically assign the extension **.PRG** so it is important, that when you create a format file you use the extension **.FMT**, if it is not used the program will not work properly.

Type : **MODIFY COMMAND B:ACUSTOM.FMT**

Press the RETURN key, the dBASEIII word processor screen will appear as shown in Figure 13–8.

SECTION 13
Creating a data entry form

dBASE Word Processor

```
CURSOR:   <-- -->          UP    DOWN      DELETE              Insert Mode:      Ins
Char:      ←   →     Line:  ↑      ↓       Char:     Del       Insert line:      ^N
Word:    Home End    Page: PgUp  PgDn      Word:     ^T        Save: ^W  Abort:Esc
Line:       ^↑ ^↓    Find:       ^KF       Line:     ^Y        Read file:        ^KR
Reformat: ^KB        Refind:     ^KL                           Write file:       ^KW
```

Figure 13-8

Now type in the ACUSTOM.FMT format file exactly as shown below:

```
**********ACUSTOM.FMT**********
@  1,1  SAY "Record Number"
@  1,17 SAY RECNO()
@  3,53 SAY "Customer Number :  " GET CUSTOMER_NO
@  5,12 SAY "Customer Name    :  " GET CUST_NAME
@  7,12 SAY "Address          :  " GET ADD_1
@  8,12 SAY "                    " GET ADD_2
@  9,12 SAY "                    " GET ADD_3
@ 10,12 SAY "Postcode         :  " GET POSTCODE
@ 12,12 SAY "Telephone Number :  " GET TEL_NO
@ 16,5  SAY " Date Account Opened :  " GET DATE
@ 16,53 SAY "Discount    :  " GET DISCOUNT
@ 19,14 SAY "Contact Name   :  " GET CONTACT
```

Now press the **Ctrl-KW** to save the file and return to the dot prompt.

In the second line of the program the command **RECNO()** was used, this command will display the current record number.

Now let's test our new format file, firstly ensure that the database file CUSTOMER.DBF is in use, if not type the following command at the dot prompt:

USE B:CUSTOMER

then press the RETURN key.

59

SECTION 13
Creating a data entry form

To tell dBASEIII the name of the screen to use you would use the **SET FORMAT TO** command, the format file that has been created is named 'ACUSTOM'. Now type:

SET FORMAT TO ACUSTOM

and then press the RETURN key. Another dot prompt will appear on the next line. Now to see what the form looks like on screen we can either use the **APPEND** or **EDIT** commands. Type **APPEND** and then press the RETURN key, the screen should then look as follows, to view more records press either the **PgDn** or the **PgUp** keys to move through the file.

```
Record Number :        11
                                         Customer Number :  C011
          Customer Name    :  SOLE GROUP
          Address          :  AIR HOUSE
                              WILLIAM ROAD
                              CHELTENHAM
          Postcode         :  GT48 3FT
          Telephone Number :  0242 573452

   Date Account Opened    :  09/08/87         Discount   :   6.00

          Contact Name     :  PAM McLACHAN
```

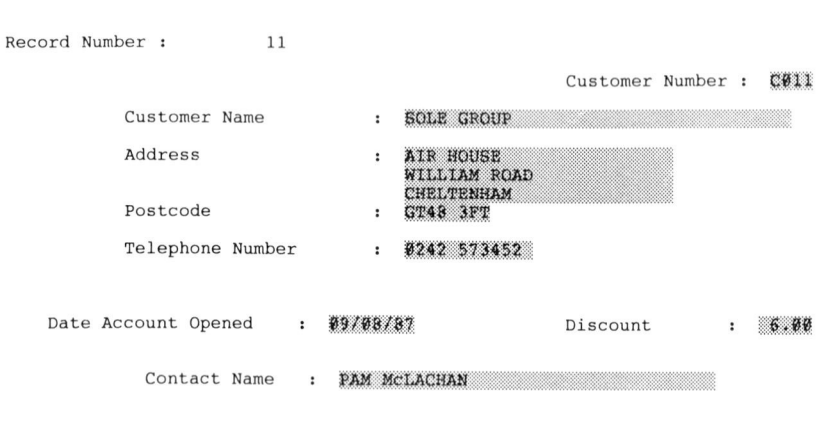

Figure 13-9

SECTION 14
Using the modify menu

When leaving the data entry form by pressing **F10** we can use the Modify menu to change a field's display and its entry characteristics. The structure of the database file will not be affected. The options available are:

Action — This option will describe whether the data in the field can be edited (Edit/GET) or the data is for (Display/SAY).

Picture Function — This option specifies a special conversion or replacement of data from the database file before it is shown on the form.

Picture Template — This option will determine what characters are allowed to be entered.

Range — This option will set a lower and upper limit on numbers that you can enter into a numeric field, i.e. a range between 500 and 2500. If the entry was outside the two figures, a message would be shown at the bottom of the screen describing the range.

On the screen showing our data entry form, move the cursor to the date field and then press **F10** to display the Modify menu which will show the information on the date field.

Move the highlighted bar to Picture Function and press RETURN, then enter **'E'** against the prompt **Function Value**, press RETURN. Now press **F10** again to return to our data entry form. Our date field will not look any different, but the date will now be shown in European standard day/month/year format not American standard month/day/year.

SECTION 15
Printing and saving the data entry form

dBASEIII Plus

Now that we have finished creating our data entry form it's time to check it by printing it. There are two methods to do this, one is by using an option from the Screen Painter Menu Bar which will let you save a text file image of the created form and can be printed at any time. The other way is to use **PrtSc**.

To save our form press **F10** to display the Screen Painter Menu Bar, then move the highlighted bar to the Exit Menu and select **Save**. When this is completed the Assistant Menu will be shown.

dBASEIII

To print out our form you will have to type the following command:

SET PRINT ON

and then press the RETURN key.
To print out our records type:

DO B:ACUSTOM

and then the records will be printed. When you have finished printing make sure you type the following command at the dot prompt:

SET PRINT OFF

and press RETURN. If you do not do this, everything that you type on the screen will be printed.

PART FIVE

Adding, displaying and editing records

■ SECTION 16
Adding records to a database file

dBASEIII Plus

More than often we will need to add records to a database file. One way in which this can be done is by using Append from the Update menu in the main Assistant menu.

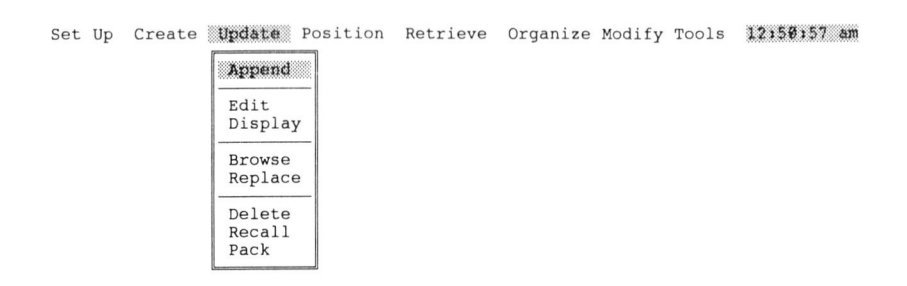

```
Set Up   Create   Update   Position   Retrieve   Organize  Modify  Tools   12:50:57 am
                  ┌─────────┐
                  │ Append  │
                  ├─────────┤
                  │ Edit    │
                  │ Display │
                  │         │
                  │ Browse  │
                  │ Replace │
                  │         │
                  │ Delete  │
                  │ Recall  │
                  │ Pack    │
                  └─────────┘










ASSIST            |<B;>|CUSTOMER              |Rec: 1/11              |Ins  |
```

Figure 16–1

When Append is selected a template screen will be shown as in Figure 9–6, it will be ready for you to enter the next record. For the purpose of this example we will use the existing CUSTOMER database file and Append the following records to it.

Select Append and press RETURN.

You will notice that the status bar will show the current record number as being EOF/8 and is ready to receive the ninth record.

Field	Record 9	Record 10	Record 11
CUST_NO	C009	C010	C011
CUST_NAME	SCRIBE SYSTEMS	K.B.A	SOLE GROUP
ADD_1	OLD MILL LANE	3 NEWTON PLACE	AIR HOUSE
ADD_2	RIVER WAY	ACTON	WILLIAM ROAD
ADD_3	OXFORD	LONDON	CHELTENHAM
POSTCODE	OX4 9BY	W3 2AB	GT48 3FT
DISCOUNT	4.0	10.0	6.0
DATE	111185	020687	090887
TEL_NO	0863 348756	01 993 497374	0242 573452
CONTACT	ROBERT OGDEN	MIKE GLOVER	PAM McLACHLAN

SECTION 16
Adding records to a database file

dBASEIII

To add records to our database file CUSTOMER using dBASEIII is very similar to dBASEIII Plus.

First ensure that the current database file in use is Customer then move the highlighted bar to the **Modify** menu and press the down arrow key, you will now be in the **Modify Database** screen. Press the down arrow key and select **Append**, a template screen will be shown as in Figure 9-6, awaiting the entry of Record No. 9.

Now enter Records 9 to 11 as previously shown in the dBASEIII Plus section, and then save the records using **Ctrl-End** keys.

■ SECTION 17
Displaying records using browse

dBASEIII Plus

We can now return to the Update menu (Figure 16–1) and move the highlighted bar down to the command Browse and then press RETURN. The screen will now show all the current records in our file CUSTOMER as shown in Figure 17–1.

```
CURSOR     <-- -->         UP   DOWN      DELETE           Insert Mode:   Ins
Char:      ← →     Record:  ↑    ↓        Char:   Del      Exit:         ^End
Field: Home End    Page:  PgUp  PgDn      Field:  ^Y       Abort:         Esc
Pan:       ^← ^→   Help:   F1             Record: ^U       Set Options: ^Home
CUST_NO  CUST_NAME----------------------- ADD_1-------------------
C011     SOLE GROUP                       AIR HOUSE




BROWSE         |<B:>|CUSTOMER             |Rec: 11/11      |         |
```

Figure 17–1

Now that we are using the Browse option we are able to look at up to seventeen records at the same time, with each record appearing on a separate line. In the case of our database file CUSTOMER we have more fields in the record than can fit on to the screen (it will only display up to 80 characters wide), the fields to the left will be shown on the screen first as Figure 17–1. To view the rest of the record press Ctrl-→ a few times and you will see new fields appearing into view from the right-hand side of the screen, by pressing Ctrl-← the fields will scroll back in the opposite direction.

Press the End key and the cursor will move one field to the right and if the Home key is pressed the cursor will move one field to the left.

If the F10 key is pressed the Browse menu bar will appear across the top of the screen.

SECTION 17
Displaying records using browse

```
CURSOR     <-- -->         UP   DOWN       DELETE          Insert Mode:   Ins
  Char:      ←   →    Record:  ↑     ↓       Char:   Del   Exit:         ^End
  Field: Home End     Page:  PgUp  PgDn      Field:    ^Y  Abort:         Esc
  Pan:      ^←^→      Help:    F1            Record:   ^U  Set Options: ^Home
CUSTNUMBER CLIENTNAME------------------ ADD1--------------------
```

Figure 17–2

To access any of the Browse menu bar, select using the left or right arrow keys and then press RETURN, each command has a specific function as described in the table below:

Browse menu

Bottom	—	Will move to the last record in the file.
Top	—	Will move to the first record in the file.
Lock	—	This will enable you to keep the fields on the left-hand side of the screen while you look across the record.
Record No.	—	Will move to a specific record.
Freeze	—	This will protect all but a selected field from editing.
Find	—	This will search for a constant, character string, or an expression. This option only appears if you've selected an index.

Table 17–1

67

■ SECTION 17
Displaying records using browse

It is also possible to add new records to the file when in Browse. First move the highlighted bar down to the last record in the file and press the down arrow (↓) key once, dBASEIII Plus will then ask:

Add new records?(Y/N)

When the screen is as shown in Figure 17-1, only a maximum of 11 records can be displayed on the screen at one time, press the F1 key and the top part of the screen will not be shown enabling 17 records to be displayed at one time.

dBASEIII

When in the **Modify Database** menu move the highlighted bar to the **Browse** menu and press the down arrow key, the screen will show part of Record No. 11 as shown below:

```
Record No.      11      customer
```

CURSOR <-- -->	UP DOWN	DELETE	Insert Mode: Ins
Char: ← →	Record: ↑ ↓	Char: Del	Exit: ^End
Field: Home End	Page: PgUp PgDn	Field: ^Y	Abort: Esc
Pan: ^← ^→		Record: ^U	Set Options: ^Home

```
CUST_NO  CUST_NAME----------------------- ADD 1-------------------
C011     SOLE GROUP                              AIR HOUSE
```

Figure 17-3

To view the rest of the Record press the **Ctrl-Right Arrow** keys to move one field at a time across the page, pressing **PgUp** will highlight the next record. To add new records press the down arrow key when the highlighted bar is on the last record (11), and a prompt will be shown at the top of the screen:

Add new records? (Y/N)

SECTION 18
Editing records

dBASEIII Plus

If we find any mistakes in our field entries we can correct them by going back to the Update menu and move the highlighted bar to the Edit option and press RETURN. The first record C001 will now be displayed on the screen, if you wish to view or edit another just press the PgDn or PgUp keys to move forward or backwards through the records.

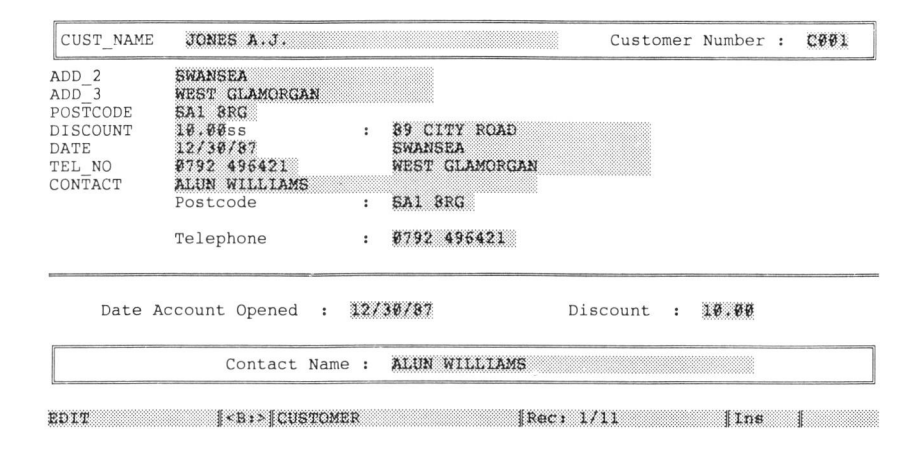

```
   CUST_NAME    JONES A.J.                        Customer Number :  C001
ADD_2           SWANSEA
ADD_3           WEST GLAMORGAN
POSTCODE        SA1 3RG
DISCOUNT        10.00ss            :  89 CITY ROAD
DATE            12/30/87              SWANSEA
TEL_NO          0792 496421           WEST GLAMORGAN
CONTACT         ALUN WILLIAMS
                Postcode           :  SA1 3RG

                Telephone          :  0792 496421

       Date Account Opened  :  12/30/87         Discount  :  10.00

              Contact Name  :  ALUN WILLIAMS

EDIT           <B:>|CUSTOMER              |Rec: 1/11        |Ins  |
```

Figure 18–1

When you have selected Edit, press PgDn until you reach record number C004, as shown in Figure 18–1, then use the down arrow key to move the cursor to the field marked DISCOUNT.

The data in the field can be overwritten or deleted to make a new entry. Now type 10.0 and press RETURN without moving the cursor from the start of the field.

Any or all of the fields can be edited in this way. When you have finished with the alteration to record number C004, press Ctrl-End to save the change in the record and also to return to the Assistant menu. If the changes that have been made to a record or records are not required to be saved press the Esc key instead of pressing Ctrl-End.

69

■ SECTION 18
Editing records

If a complete record had to be deleted from our database file, you would then first, select a record and when it is on screen press Ctrl-U to mark that record for deletion, this record is now marked and is indicated on the status bar. Now press Ctrl-End to leave Edit and return to the Assistant menu.

To date all that has been done is to mark a record for deletion, it can still be displayed, edited or copied. To remove the marked record from the database file we have to use the Pack option from the Update menu.

Select Pack and press RETURN, the marked record will now be permanently removed from the database file, a message:

xx records copied

will now appear, this will indicate that there are now xx records in the database file. Now press any other key to continue.

Another method of editing is to use the Delete option in the Update menu. When using the Delete option, it will let you mark any number of records that have something in common, i.e. all records that have a discount level below 5%. To do this select Delete and press RETURN, a scope/search menu will appear, select **Build a search condition** option, once selected a menu of all the fields will be shown as in Figure 17–2.

Now move the highlighted bar to the DISCOUNT field, press RETURN and another menu will appear, this will show relational operators, move the highlighted bar to < **Less Than**.

What has happened now is that we have told dBASEIII Plus that we want all records which are less than a specified value to be deleted. dBASEIII Plus will now prompt you to:

Enter a numeric value (see Figure 18–2)

Now type 5.0 and then select **No more conditions**, then select **Execute the command**. dBASEIII Plus will now mark all the appropriate records that are to be deleted, and will then inform you that **x records deleted**.

■ SECTION 18
Editing records

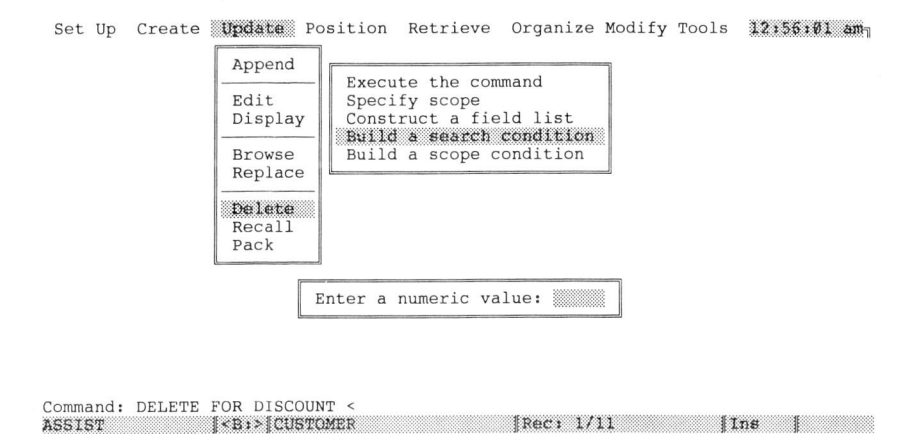

```
Set Up   Create   Update   Position   Retrieve   Organize Modify Tools   12:56:01 am
                 ┌─────────┬─────────────────────────────┐
                 │ Append  │ Execute the command         │
                 │         │ Specify scope               │
                 │ Edit    │ Construct a field list      │
                 │ Display │ Build a search condition    │
                 │         │ Build a scope condition     │
                 │ Browse  └─────────────────────────────┘
                 │ Replace │
                 ├─────────┤
                 │ Delete  │
                 │ Recall  │
                 │ Pack    │
                 └─────────┘
                           ┌──────────────────────────────┐
                           │ Enter a numeric value:       │
                           └──────────────────────────────┘

Command: DELETE FOR DISCOUNT <
ASSIST        <B:>CUSTOMER              Rec: 1/11          Ins
```

Figure 18–2

If you now want to remove the records, select the Pack option from the Update menu. This will ensure that the records are deleted from your database file CUSTOMER.

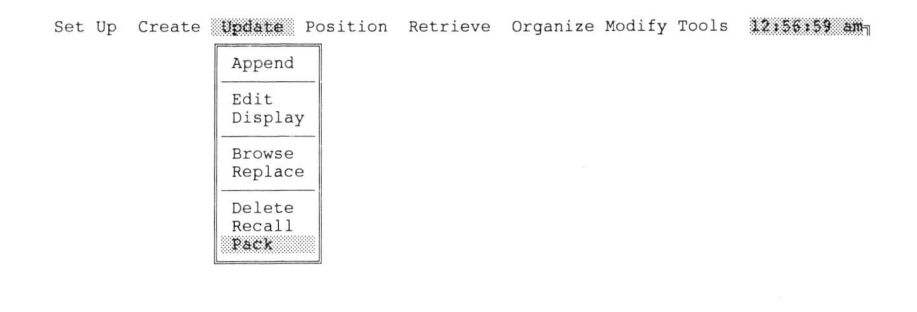

```
Set Up   Create   Update   Position   Retrieve   Organize Modify Tools   12:56:59 am
                 ┌─────────┐
                 │ Append  │
                 ├─────────┤
                 │ Edit    │
                 │ Display │
                 ├─────────┤
                 │ Browse  │
                 │ Replace │
                 ├─────────┤
                 │ Delete  │
                 │ Recall  │
                 │ Pack    │
                 └─────────┘




ASSIST        <B:>CUSTOMER              Rec: 1/11          Ins
```

Figure 18–3

71

SECTION 18
Editing records

dBASEIII

To edit in dBASEIII move the highlighted bar to the **Edit** menu in the **Modify Database** screen, now press the down arrow key and the screen should be as in Figure 18–1, follow the instructions in the dBASEIII Plus section, try editing and then back.

To delete a record, press the **Ctrl-U** and the screen will look as in Figure 18–4. If we want to remove the marked record from our database file exit to the **Edit** menu and return to the **dBASEIII Assistant** menu and then move the highlighted bar to the **Organize** menu. Press the down arrow key and select **Pack** by moving the highlighted bar to **Pack**, then press RETURN. A message telling you the number of records copied will be displayed on the screen.

```
Record No.     11                      *DEL*
```

CURSOR <-- -->	UP DOWN	DELETE	Insert Mode: Ins
Char:	Field:	Char: Del	Exit: ^End
Word: Home End	Page: PgUp PgDn	Field: ^Y	Abort: Esc
		Record: ^U	Text: ^Home

```
CUST_NO      C011
CUST_NAME    SOLE GROUP
ADD_1        AIR HOUSE
ADD_2        WILLIAM ROAD
ADD_3        CHELTENHAM
POSTCODE     GT48 3FT
DISCOUNT     6.00
DATE         09/08/87
TEL_NO       0242 573452
CONTACT      PAM McLACHAN
```

Figure 18–4

PART SIX

Processing records

SECTION 19
Locating a record

dBASEIII Plus

In dBASEIII Plus we are able to call up any specific record that we require, to do this we need to be in the Assistant menu. Move the highlighted bar to Position and then select **Goto Record**, we are now given three options to select from as in Figure 19–1. Select the option Record and press RETURN.

You will now be prompted to:

Enter a numeric value:

Enter 3 and press the RETURN key, the status bar will now indicate that the new record number is now record 3.

```
Set Up   Create   Update   Position   Retrieve   Organize Modify Tools   12:58:51 am

                          Seek
                          ─────────         TOP
                          Locate            BOTTOM
                          Continue          RECORD

                          Skip
                          Goto Record




Command: GOTO
ASSIST          |<B:>|CUSTOMER              |Rec: 1/11          |Ins  |
```

Figure 19–1

Another way of going through the records in our database file is to use the Skip command in the Position menu in the Assistant menu.

Select Skip and press RETURN, you will then be asked to enter a numeric value. Enter 2 and if the current record is 3, record 5 will become the current record. It is also possible to enter a negative value, if you enter –3 and the current record is number 5, record 2 will become the current record.

■ SECTION 19
Locating a record

Instead of using the Skip and Goto options, we can use the Locate option. This command will help us to find records when we do not know their number especially when the database file is very large. Let's look at this command in a bit more detail as it is very useful. Select Locate in the Position menu and then select **Build a search condition**. A submenu of all the fields in our file CUSTOMER will be shown, see Figure 19–2.

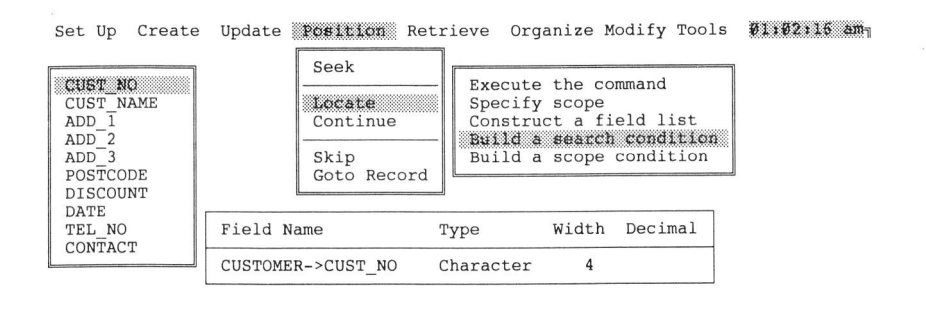

```
Set Up   Create   Update   Position   Retrieve   Organize Modify Tools   01:02:16 am

CUST_NO              Seek
CUST_NAME                              Execute the command
ADD_1                Locate            Specify scope
ADD_2                Continue          Construct a field list
ADD_3                                  Build a search condition
POSTCODE             Skip              Build a scope condition
DISCOUNT             Goto Record
DATE
TEL_NO               Field Name        Type          Width    Decimal
CONTACT
                     CUSTOMER->CUST_NO  Character     4


Command: LOCATE
ASSIST          |<B:>|CUSTOMER              |Rec: 2/11            |Ins   |
```

Figure 19–2

Now select the DISCOUNT field and press RETURN and a further submenu will be shown of relational operators, see Figure 19–3. Move the highlighted bar <= **Less Than or Equal To**, dBASEIII Plus will then prompt you to to enter a number. Enter 3.0 and press RETURN, now select **No more conditions** and then move the highlighted bar up to **Execute the command**, press RETURN and the Locate operation will take place. The number of the first record with a discount of less than or equal to 3.0 will be shown on the action line, in this case it will be record 7.

75

■ SECTION 19
Locating a record

```
Set Up   Create   Update   Position   Retrieve   Organize Modify Tools   01:03:23 am
```

```
Record =        7
ASSIST          |<B:>|CUSTOMER                |Rec: 2/11              |Ins   |
```

Figure 19–3

Now press any key to continue, and then open the Update menu selecting the Edit command to display the record that we have just located in our database file. Now return to the Position menu, but now select the **Continue** command. dBASEIII Plus will now display on the action line – **End of LOCATE scope**, if there had been any more records with a discount field of less than or equal to 3.0 the next one would have shown on the action line and could have been viewed in the Edit mode.

76

■ SECTION 19
Locating a record

dBASEIII

In dBASEIII we can use the commands **Locate** and **Go** to locate a record. Firstly make sure that the **dBASEIII Assistant** menu is on screen, then move the highlighted bar to the **Position** menu and press the down arrow key to bring up the **Position Database Pointer** screen, move the highlighted bar to the **Locate** command and the screen should look as in Figure 19–4.

```
                       Position Database Pointer                     READY
Find       Locate      Continue      Skip        Go      Modify      Retrieve
┌─────────────────────────────────────────────────────────────────────────┐
│Locate a record that satisfies condition.                                │
└─────────────────────────────────────────────────────────────────────────┘


┌─────────────────────────────────────────────────────────────────────────┐
│                              LOCATE                                     │
│ LOCATE finds the first record in the database matching a given condition.│
│ Unlike the FIND command,  LOCATE does not use an index file.  It searches│
│ the database file in its natural order.                                 │
│                                                                         │
│         Command Format:   LOCATE [<scope>] [FOR <condition>]            │
│                                                                         │
└─────────────────────────────────────────────────────────────────────────┘



Command: Locate
```

Figure 19–4

SECTION 19
Locating a record

Press the down arrow key and move the highlighted bar to **Record** and then press the RETURN key, dBASEIII will then prompt you:

Enter a Numeric value:

Enter 3 and press RETURN, then press the right arrow key and the screen will look as follows:

```
                        Position Database Pointer
Find       Locate       Continue    Skip      Go       Modify         Retrieve
Select conditional statement if desired

Record =     3
```

Command: Locate RECORD 3

Figure 19-5

To see the record, exit the menu and return to the **dBASEIII Assistant** menu and select the **Retrieve** menu, press the down arrow key and then select **Display**, press the right arrow key twice and the screen should look as in Figure 19-6.

■ SECTION 19
Locating a record

Now select the following fields:

```
CUST_NO
CUST_NAME
DISCOUNT
TEL_NO
```

and when the fields have been selected press the right arrow key. Record 3 will now be positioned on screen and should look as follows:

```
Record#   CUST_NO  CUST_NAME              DISCOUNT  TEL_NO
     3    C003_    COMCOL LTD_                4.50  0659597821
```

```
                            Retrieve and Present Information
Display      Sum       Average      Count    Label    Report        Position
Select Field names - Position using  /  ARROW KEYS  -  Select using ENTER

                        Field Name    Field Type   Width   Dec. #
                        CUST_NO       Character      4
                        CUST_NAME     Character     36
                        ADD_1         Character     25
                        ADD_2         Character     25
                        ADD_3         Character     25
                        POSTCODE      Character      8
                        DISCOUNT      Numeric        5     2
                        DATE          Date           8
                        TEL_NO        Character     12
                        CONTACT       Character     35
```

Command: Display

Figure 19-6

The **Skip** command can also be used in the same way as dBASEIII Plus.

If you use the **Go** command in the **Position Database Pointer** screen, you will be able to move to the **TOP** record, i.e. move to the first record in the file, the **BOTTOM** record, or the last record in the file, it is also possible to move to any specified record number.

■ SECTION 20
Indexing records

dBASEIII Plus

At present the records in our database file CUSTOMER are in customer number order, it would be helpful to rearrange this file into say, alphabetical order on the customer name or by what discount they receive. This can be done by indexing the records.

Firstly go to the Assistant menu, if you are not there already, then open the **Organize Menu** and then select **Index**. dBASEIII Plus will then prompt you to **Enter an index key expression**, press **F10** and a submenu of all the fields in the file CUSTOMER will be shown, see Figure 20–1. Move the highlighted bar to CUST_NAME and press RETURN.

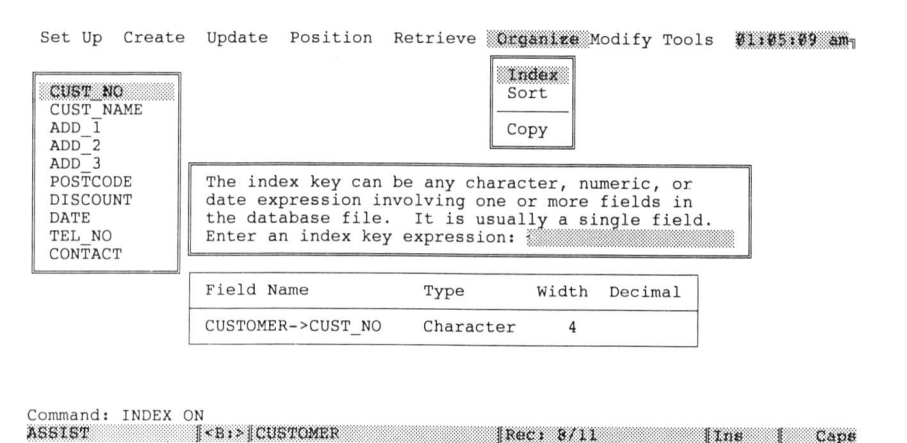

```
Set Up   Create   Update   Position   Retrieve   Organize  Modify Tools    01:05:09 am

┌─────────────┐              ┌─────────┐
│ CUST_NO     │              │ Index   │
│ CUST_NAME   │              │ Sort    │
│ ADD_1       │              ├─────────┤
│ ADD_2       │              │ Copy    │
│ ADD_3       │     ┌────────┴─────────┴──────────────────────────┐
│ POSTCODE    │     │ The index key can be any character, numeric, or │
│ DISCOUNT    │     │ date expression involving one or more fields in │
│ DATE        │     │ the database file.  It is usually a single field. │
│ TEL_NO      │     │ Enter an index key expression:                  │
│ CONTACT     │     └─────────────────────────────────────────────────┘
└─────────────┘
                    ┌─────────────────────────────────────────────┐
                    │ Field Name           Type      Width  Decimal │
                    │ CUSTOMER->CUST_NO    Character    4          │
                    └─────────────────────────────────────────────┘

Command: INDEX ON
ASSIST         |<B:>|CUSTOMER               |Rec: 8/11          |Ins  |  Caps
```

Figure 20–1

■ SECTION 20
Indexing records

The field CUST_NAME will be shown against the prompt, **Enter an index key expression**, press RETURN and select B drive by moving the highlighted bar to B, then press RETURN again.

dBASE will then prompt you to **Enter a file name**, type the word **NAME** and press RETURN. At the bottom of the screen you will then see **100% indexed 11 Records indexed**.

Before we check our new file 'NAME' we will create another indexed file called PERCENT. To do this open the **Organize menu** and open **Index**, press **F10** and move the highlighted bar to the DISCOUNT field. Now press RETURN twice and select drive 'B', enter PERCENT against the prompt asking for a name of a file, press RETURN and you will see the previous message appear on the screen again **100% indexed 11 Records indexed**.

Now that we have indexed the two files the first one on customer name and the second one on the discount field, let's now list them to see them in their indexed form.

Return to the Assistant menu and then move the highlighted bar to the Retrieve menu, select List and then press RETURN, the List submenu will appear as shown in Figure 12–1. Move the highlighted bar to 'Construct a field list' and press the RETURN key, we will now see another submenu of the fields in the file CUSTOMER.

Select the following fields by pressing the RETURN key by each one:

```
CUST_NO
CUST_NAME
DISCOUNT
TEL_NO
```

■ SECTION 20
Indexing records

Now leave the menu by pressing the right arrow key and then move the highlighted bar to **Execute the command** and press RETURN. Direct the output to the screen and we will see our records listed as shown in the figure below:

```
Record#   CUST_NO   CUST_NAME            DISCOUNT   TEL_NO
     7    C007      XYZ SYSTEMS LTD      2.50       080426 492
     9    C009      SCRIBE SYSTEMS       4.00       0863 348756
     3    C003      COMCOL LTD.          4.50       0659 597821
     6    C006      MANNS LIMITED        4.50       0734 7482
     5    C005      SAA LTD              5.00       0782 64921
    11    C011      SOLE GROUP           6.00       0242 573452
     2    C002      LUBRICAL LTD.        7.50       0721 433346
     4    C004      OKONI UK. LTD        8.50       01 541 49621
     1    C001      JONES A.J.           10.00      0792 496421
     8    C008      AMAD LTD             10.00      01 751 4311
    10    C010      K.B.A                10.00      01 993497374
```

Figure 20-2

As we can see from the above listing our records have been indexed on the DISCOUNT field starting from the smallest discount to the largest discount, this could be very useful in a very large Customer Record File where there were many accounts and a wide range of discounts offered. By indexing you would be able to look at a group of customers that you were giving a certain percentage discount and not have to go through the file looking for the customers who had that discount.

Now you have looked at the PERCENT file we should also check the NAME file, to do this go back to the Assistant menu and move the highlighted bar to the Set Up menu. Select Database file and press RETURN then select drive B. Press RETURN and then again to accept the file CUSTOMER, dBASEIII Plus will then prompt:

Is the file indexed?[Y/N]

■ SECTION 20
Indexing records

Type 'Y' and a submenu of indexed files will appear, as shown in Figure 20–3, move the highlighted bar to the file NAME and press RETURN and the exit the menu.

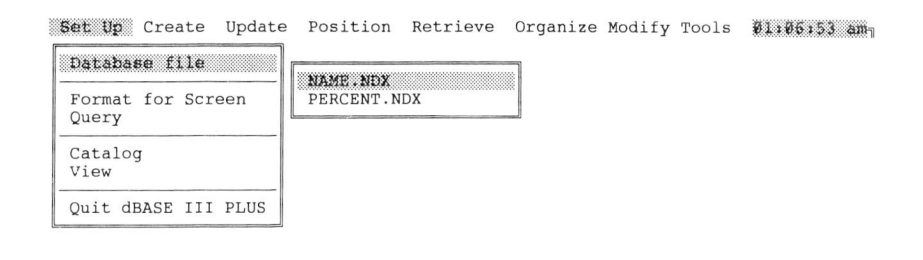

```
Set Up   Create  Update  Position  Retrieve  Organize Modify Tools   01:06:53 am
┌─────────────────────────┐
│ Database file           │
│ ┌───────────────────────┤ ┌──────────────┐
│ Format for Screen       │ │ NAME.NDX     │
│ Query                   │ │ PERCENT.NDX  │
├─────────────────────────┤ └──────────────┘
│ Catalog                 │
│ View                    │
├─────────────────────────┤
│ Quit dBASE III PLUS     │
└─────────────────────────┘


Command: USE B:CUSTOMER INDEX
ASSIST        |<B:>|CUSTOMER              |Rec: 1/11           |Ins  |  Caps
```

Figure 20–3

Return to the Assistant menu and then move the highlighted bar to the Retrieve menu, select List and then press RETURN, the List submenu will appear as shown in Figure 12–1. Move the highlighted bar to 'Construct a field list' and press the RETURN key, we will now see another submenu of the fields in the file CUSTOMER.

SECTION 20
Indexing records

Select the following fields by pressing the RETURN key by each one:

    CUST_NO
    CUST_NAME
    DISCOUNT
    TEL_NO

Now leave the menu by pressing the right arrow key and then move the highlighted bar to **Execute the command** and press RETURN. Direct the output to the screen and we will see our records listed as shown in the figure below:

```
Record#  CUST_NO  CUST_NAME            DISCOUNT   TEL_NO
     8   C008     AMAD LTD             10.00      01 751 4311
     3   C003     COMCOL LTD.           4.50      0659 597821
     1   C001     JONES A.J.           10.00      0792 496421
    10   C010     K.B.A                10.00      01 993497374
     2   C002     LUBRICAL LTD.         7.50      0721 433346
     6   C006     MANNS LIMITED         4.50      0734 7482
     4   C004     OKONI UK. LTD         8.50      01 541 49621
     5   C005     SAA LTD               5.00      0782 64921
     9   C009     SCRIBE SYSTEMS        4.00      0863 348756
    11   C011     SOLE GROUP            6.00      0242 573452
     7   C007     XYZ SYSTEMS LIMITED   2.50      080426 492
```

Figure 20–4

This listing is completely different to the first one, this one has been indexed in alphabetical order on the customer's name. Again this could be very useful, especially say for a mailshot where you only want to send information out to the companies whose names start with the letters A to D.

■ SECTION 20
Indexing records

dBASEIII

To index records in dBASEIII we can nearly follow the same procedures as dBASEIII Plus.

```
Select   — Organize menu and press the RETURN key.
Select   — Index and press the RETURN key.
Type     — NAME at the prompt for the name of the file and press
           the RETURN key.
```

The screen should look as follows:

```
                        Organize Database
Index                Sort              Copy                    Pack
Enter key expression:

                        Field Name    Field Type    Width    Dec. #
                        CUST_NO       Character       4
                        CUST_NAME     Character      36
                        ADD_1         Character      25
                        ADD_2         Character      25
                        ADD_3         Character      25
                        POSTCODE      Character       8
                        DISCOUNT      Numeric         5        2
                        DATE          Date            8
                        TEL_NO        Character      12
                        CONTACT       Character      35

Command: Index
```

Figure 20-5

Enter CUST_NAME against the prompt **Enter by expression** and press the RETURN key. dBASEIII will then display message '11 records indexed'. Now as in the dBASEIII Plus section create another indexed file named PERCENT.

SECTION 21
Copying records

dBASEIII Plus

Before we look at sorting records we will create another database file to work on, go back to the Assistant menu and create the following file which we call **CUSTACC**.

Field Name	Type	Width	Dec
CUST_NO	Character	4	
CUST_NAME	Character	35	
DISCOUNT	Numeric	5	
CRE_LIM	Numeric	8	2
AM_OWED	Numeric	8	2
SPEND_T/D	Numeric	8	2
SPEND_L/Y	Numeric	8	2

Now enter the following information into the file, the CUST_NO, CUST_NAME and DISCOUNT fields are the same as in our CUSTOMER file.

	Record 1	Record 2	Record 3	Record 4
CRE_LIM	1000.00	1500.00	500.00	1000.00
AM_OWED	95.42	621.42	0.00	329.99
SPEND_T/D	1497.56	4641.89	895.41	1948.45
SPEND_L/Y	8943.18	18340.00	2041.66	6325.62

	Record 5	Record 6	Record 7	Record 8
CRE_LIM	2000.00	1250.00	1750.00	1000.00
AM_OWED	899.11	625.49	946.46	49.67
SPEND_T/D	4280.09	5341.21	4102.22	3241.46
SPEND_L/Y	25400.00	11490.01	10000.00	9629.98

	Record 9	Record 10	Record 11
CRE_LIM	500.00	500.00	3000.00
AM_OWED	49.67	121.75	1246.29
SPEND_T/D	989.46	1256.33	12390.64
SPEND_L/Y	2340.11	3400.50	32480.48

■ SECTION 21
Copying records

When all the information has been entered, use the List command and select the following fields, CUST_NO, DISCOUNT, CRE_LIM, AM_OWED, SPEN_T/D and SPEND_L/Y. When you have done this execute the command and check that your screen is as follows:

```
Record#  CUST_NO  DISCOUNT  CRE_LIM   AM_OWED  SPEND_TD  SPEND_LY
     1   C008       10.00   1000.00     49.67   3241.46   9629.98
     2   C003        4.50    500.00      0.00    895.41   2041.66
     3   C001       10.00   1000.00     95.42   1497.56   8943.18
     4   C010       10.00    500.00    121.75   1256.33   3400.50
     5   C002        7.50   1500.00    621.42   4641.89  18340.00
     6   C006        4.50   1250.00    625.49   5341.21  11490.01
     7   COO4        8.50   1000.00    329.99   1948.45   6325.62
     8   C005        5.00   2000.00    899.11   4280.09  25400.00
     9   C009        4.00    500.00     49.67    989.46   2340.11
    10   C011        6.00   3000.00   1246.29  12390.64  32480.48
    11   C007        2.50   1750.00    946.46   4102.22  10000.00
```

Figure 21-1

The way that we have just used is very time consuming, to save time in creating our new database file dBASEIII Plus will allow us to copy fields from one database file to another. In our first database file 'CUSTOMER' we used the following fields:

    CUST_NO
    CUST_NAME
    DISCOUNT

These are the three fields that we require from CUSTOMER for our new file CUSTACC. Against these fields we entered information which would be very time consuming to enter in again. To avoid this go to the Assistant menu and move the highlighted bar to the **Organize** menu and then select **Copy**, press RETURN. dBASEIII Plus will then prompt:

Enter the name of the file:

87

■ SECTION 21
Copying records

Enter CUSTOM and press RETURN, a submenu will then be shown, move the highlighted bar to **Construct a field list** and press RETURN.

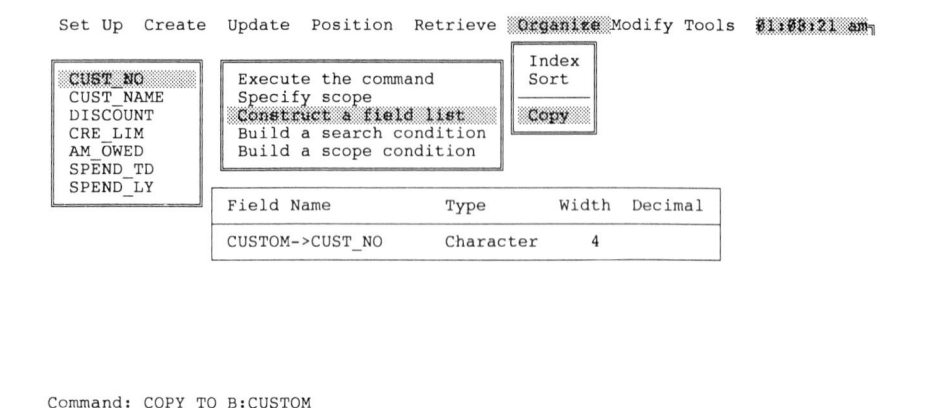

```
     Set Up   Create   Update   Position   Retrieve   Organize Modify Tools   01:03:21 am

    CUST_NO      Execute the command      Index
    CUST_NAME    Specify scope            Sort
    DISCOUNT     Construct a field list
    CRE_LIM      Build a search condition   Copy
    AM_OWED      Build a scope condition
    SPEND_TD
    SPEND_LY
                 Field Name         Type        Width   Decimal

                 CUSTOM->CUST_NO    Character     4


Command: COPY TO B:CUSTOM
ASSIST          |<B:>|CUSTOM                    |Rec: 1/11              |Ins   |   Caps
```

Figure 21-2

The screen should now look as in Figure 20-2, now select CUST_NO, CUST_NAME and DISCOUNT from the field list of the file CUSTOMER, once selected leave the menu and move the highlighted bar to **Execute the command** and press RETURN. A message will appear at the bottom of the screen, **11 records copied**.

■ SECTION 21
Copying records

Press any key to continue then move the highlighted bar to the **Modify** menu and select **Database file**, press RETURN and the screen will look as follows:

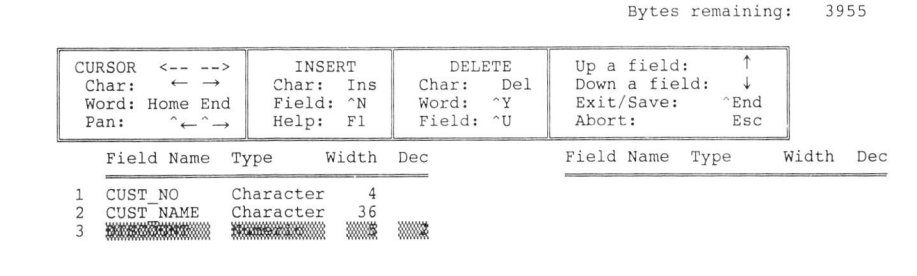

```
                                                  Bytes remaining:    3955

 CURSOR    <-- -->  │   INSERT       │    DELETE      │ Up a field:      ↑
 Char:      ← →     │ Char:   Ins    │ Char:    Del   │ Down a field:    ↓
 Word: Home End     │ Field:  ^N     │ Word:    ^Y    │ Exit/Save:     ^End
 Pan:    ^←^→       │ Help:   F1     │ Field:   ^U    │ Abort:          Esc

       Field Name   Type     Width  Dec         Field Name   Type     Width  Dec

    1  CUST_NO      Character   4
    2  CUST_NAME    Character  36
    3  ▓▓▓▓▓▓▓▓     ▓▓▓▓▓▓▓▓  ▓▓▓   ▓▓
```

Figure 21–3

Move the highlighted bar by pressing the down arrow key three times, and the bar will now be in field four. Now enter the new fields and save when you have completed entering.

When back in the Assistant menu select the **Update** menu, then select **Append** and press RETURN. Use the **PgUp** key to return the first record of your new database file. Enter the new information in our newly created fields, when finished in the normal way.

■ SECTION 21
Copying records

dBASEIII

Move the highlighted bar to the **Organize** menu and press the down arrow key and then select **Copy**, the screen should look as follows:

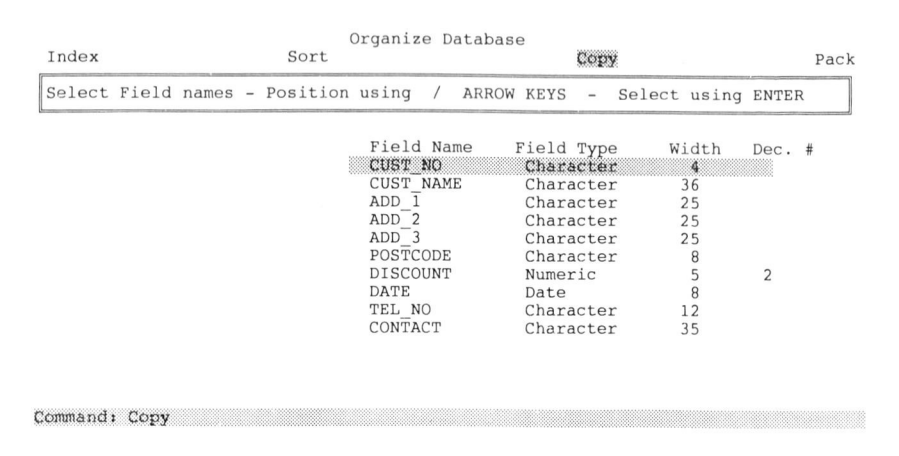

```
                        Organize Database
Index              Sort                    Copy                    Pack
Select Field names - Position using  /  ARROW KEYS  -  Select using ENTER

                        Field Name    Field Type    Width    Dec.  #
                        CUST_NO       Character       4
                        CUST_NAME     Character      36
                        ADD_1         Character      25
                        ADD_2         Character      25
                        ADD_3         Character      25
                        POSTCODE      Character       8
                        DISCOUNT      Numeric         5       2
                        DATE          Date            8
                        TEL_NO        Character      12
                        CONTACT       Character      35



Command: Copy
```

Figure 21-4

Press the down arrow key and the select the following fields:

    CUST_NO
    CUST_NAME
    DISCOUNT

Now press the right arrow key to move onto the next selection. dBASEIII will then ask for the name of the file, type **CUSTOM** and press the RETURN key. Press the right arrow key and dBASEIII will then display the message – **11 records copied**.

■ SECTION 21
Copying records

Press any key to continue, then return to the **dBASEIII Assistant** screen and select the **Set Up** menu then the **Use** command, drive B and then select the database file CUSTOM.DBF, press the RETURN key and answer 'N' to the index prompt. Now select the **Utilities** menu, as in Figure 21–5. Press the down arrow key and move the highlighted bar to **Modify structure**.

```
                         File Utilities                      READY
Set Drive    Copy File    Dir     Rename     Erase      Modify Structure
┌─────────────────────────────────────────────────────────────────────┐
│Modify database structure.                                           │
└─────────────────────────────────────────────────────────────────────┘


┌─────────────────────────────────────────────────────────────────────┐
│                        MODIFY STRUCTURE                             │
│  MODIFY STRUCTURE allows you to change the structure of a database  file.
│  Information  in the database  file is preserved where field  names  remain
│  the same.
│
│           Command Format:   MODIFY STRUCTURE [file name]
│
└─────────────────────────────────────────────────────────────────────┘



Command: Modify
```

Figure 21–5

Move the highlighted bar by pressing the down arrow key three times and the blank field number 4 will be displayed. Now enter the new fields as given in the dBASEIII Plus section, and then save the new file by pressing **Ctrl-End**.

Now move back to the **dBASEIII Assistant** screen and select **Modify** menu, press the down arrow key and select the **Append** command. Use the **PgUp** key to return to Record No. 1. Notice that the information for the first three fields has been copied as well as the field names. Enter the data shown in the dBASEIII Plus section. When completed, press the **Ctrl-W** keys to save.

91

■ SECTION 22
Sorting records

dBASEIII Plus

When a database file is sorted, the records in the file are rearranged in the order that you will specify. Make sure that you are in the Assistant menu and move the highlighted bar to the **Organize** menu and then select **Sort** and press RETURN, we will be shown a field submenu of our file as in Figure 22–1.

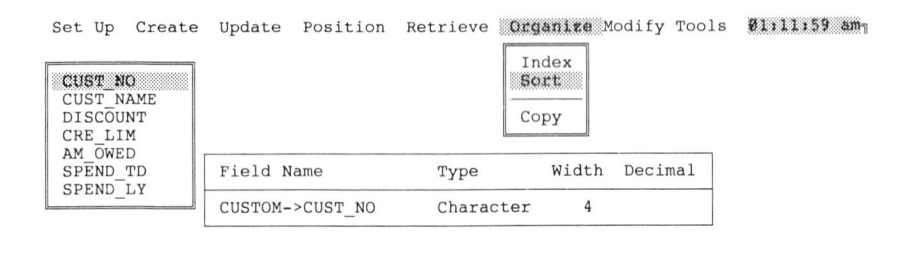

```
Set Up   Create   Update   Position   Retrieve   Organize  Modify  Tools   01:11:59 am

CUST_NO                                    Index
CUST_NAME                                  Sort
DISCOUNT                                   Copy
CRE_LIM
AM_OWED
SPEND_TD      Field Name          Type        Width   Decimal
SPEND_LY
              CUSTOM->CUST_NO     Character     4




Command: SORT ON
ASSIST           |<B:>|CUSTOM                |Rec: EOF/11         |Ins   |   Caps
```

Figure 22–1

This time we will Sort our file using the AM_OWED field. Select AM_OWED and then exit the menu using the right arrow key, then select the B drive and press RETURN. dBASEIII Plus will then prompt:

Enter the name of the file:

Enter OWED and press the RETURN key. At the bottom of the screen the message – **100% Sorted 11 Records sorted** will appear.

■ SECTION 22
Sorting records

To check that the file 'OWED' has been created move the highlighted bar to the Set Up menu and select Database file and then select the B drive, the screen should look as in Figure 22–2. Now select the database file OWED.DBF and then answer the prompt **Is the file indexed? [Y/N]** with 'N'. OWED will now appear on the status line as the database file in use.

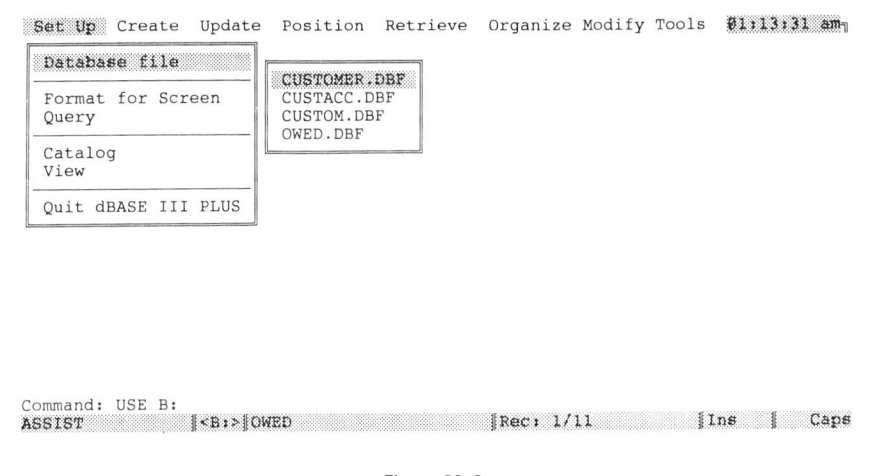

```
Set Up   Create  Update  Position  Retrieve  Organize Modify Tools   #1:13:31 am
┌─────────────────────────┐
│ Database file           │
├─────────────────────────┤  ┌──────────────┐
│ Format for Screen       │  │ CUSTOMER.DBF │
│ Query                   │  │ CUSTACC.DBF  │
├─────────────────────────┤  │ CUSTOM.DBF   │
│ Catalog                 │  │ OWED.DBF     │
│ View                    │  └──────────────┘
├─────────────────────────┤
│ Quit dBASE III PLUS     │
└─────────────────────────┘




Command: USE B:
ASSIST          |<B:>|OWED                    |Rec: 1/11             |Ins  |   Caps
```

Figure 22–2

Move the highlighted bar to the **Retrieve** menu and select **List** and press RETURN. Select **Construct a field list**, press RETURN.

SECTION 22
Sorting records

Now select the following from the field submenu by pressing the RETURN key by each one:

    CUST_NO
    DISCOUNT
    CRE_LIM
    AM_OWED
    SPEND_TD
    SPEND_LY

Leave the menu and move the highlighted bar to **Execute the command** and answer 'N' to the printer prompt unless you require a printed list of the sorted file. The screen should now look as follows:

```
Record#  CUST_NO  DISCOUNT  CRE_LIM   AM_OWED  SPEND_TD  SPEND_LY
     1   C003       4.50     500.00      0.00    895.41   2041.66
     2   C009       4.00     500.00     49.67    989.46   2340.11
     3   C001      10.00    1000.00     95.42   1497.56   8943.18
     4   C010      10.00     500.00    121.75   1256.33   3400.50
     5   C004       8.50    1000.00    329.99   1948.45   6325.62
     6   C002       7.50    1500.00    621.42   4641.89  18340.00
     7   C006       4.50    1250.00    625.49   5341.89  11490.01
     8   C005       5.00    2000.00    899.11   4280.09  25400.00
     9   C007       2.50    1750.00    946.00   4102.22  10000.00
    10   C008      10.00    1000.00    989.46   3241.46   9629.98
    11   C011       6.00    3000.00   1246.29  12390.64  32480.48
```

Figure 22-3

We could have done a sort on any of the fields in our database file, for instance we could have sorted our file on the field SPEND_TD.

To arrange our files in the order that we require we can either **Sort** or **Index** them, when we use the sort command, reports will print far more quickly from a sort file. Also when using the sort command it is possible to sort in descending as well as ascending order.

■ SECTION 22
Sorting records

When you use the **Index** command on a database file it has one very distinct advantage over a database that has been sorted and that is the index order will be maintained when you add further records or change them but with a sorted file this will not happen. You would have to resort the file after any changes had been made.

Also an indexed file will require less disk space and indexing will proceed far quicker than using the sort command.

dBASEIII

Select the **Organize** menu and then select **Sort**, the screen will then be as Figure 22–4.

```
                        Organize Database                       READY
   Index              Sort                Copy                    Pack
┌─────────────────────────────────────────────────────────────────────┐
│ Sort records into ascending or descending order.                    │
└─────────────────────────────────────────────────────────────────────┘


   ┌─────────────────────────────────────────────────────────────────┐
   │                              SORT                               │
   │                                                                 │
   │ SORT  allows   you   to sequence a database file  in either     │
   │ ascending  or descending order  on one or more fields.  Sort    │
   │ physically reorders  the database  file while INDEX creates a   │
   │ separate key file without  changing the database file.   If     │
   │ requested,  case is ignored and a dictionary sort results.      │
   │ The  "/" character preceding the "A", "D" and "C" without an    │
   │ intervening space is a part of the command structure and is     │
   │ typed as part of  the command.  The "/" character between       │
   │ "/A" and "/B" indicates  you must choose one or the other and   │
   │ is not typed as part of the command.                            │
   │                                                                 │
   │ Command Format: SORT TO <new file> ON <field1> [/A / /D [/C]]   │
   │          [,<field2>[/A / /D [/C>]],..] [<scope>] [FOR <condition>] │
   └─────────────────────────────────────────────────────────────────┘
Command: Sort
```

Figure 22–4

95

SECTION 22
Sorting records

Press the down arrow key and a list of all the fields will be displayed, we will now sort the file using the AM_OWED field. Move the highlighted bar to the AM_OWED field and press the RETURN key to select it, press the right arrow key and then:

Type: **OWED** at the file name prompt and then press RETURN.

Press the right arrow key and a message will be shown – **100% Sorted 11 Records sorted**. We now have a file named OWED.DBF saved on disk. To check that the file has been sorted correctly go back to the **Set Up Environment** screen and select **Use**, then drive B and then the file OWED.DBF, answer 'N' to the index prompt.

To check the file select the **Retrieve** menu and then **Display**. Now select the same fields as in the dBASEIII Plus section and you should end up with a listing as in Figure 22–3.

■ SECTION 23
Counting records

dBASEIII Plus

An important function of dBASEIII Plus is its ability to summarize data. For example we might need to know how many customers in our database file OWED.DBF owe more than £625.00 and then the total amount owed by these customers, then the average amount owed by all the customers in the file.

To find out how many customers, first move the highlighted bar to the **Retrieve** menu and select **Count**, press the RETURN key and move the highlighted bar to **Build a search condition**. Press RETURN and move the highlighted bar to AM_OWED, the screen should look as in Figure 23–1, press the RETURN key and then > **Greater than** and then enter 625.00 against the prompt for a numeric value, press RETURN twice. Now move the highlighted bar to **Execute the command** and press the RETURN key and the message **4 records** will appear at the bottom of the screen. Press any key to continue.

Now let's look at the amount owed by those customers. Move the highlighted bar to **Sum**, press RETURN, select **Construct a field list**, move the highlighted bar to AM_OWED, press the right arrow key to exit menu. Now select **Build a search condition** and select the field AM_OWED again and then > **Greater than**, enter 625.00 again and execute the command. dBASEIII Plus will then display at the bottom of the screen:

```
    4 records summed
AM_OWED
4706.35
```

Now to find the average, move the highlighted bar to **Average**, select **Construct a field list** and then AM_OWED, press the right arrow key and then select **Execute the command**. dBASEIII Plus will then display:

```
    11 records averaged
AM_OWED
538.60
```

We have now found out how many customers owed more than £625.00.

The total owed by those customers.

The average amount owed by all the customers.

97

■ SECTION 23
Counting records

All these commands are very useful, they could be used in a wages record file, say for searching for employees who earn more than a certain amount and are female or perhaps their average salary.

dBASEIII

Move the highlighted bar to the **Retrieve** menu in the **dBASEIII Assistant** screen and then press the down arrow key and move the highlighted bar to the **Count** command, the screen should now look as below:

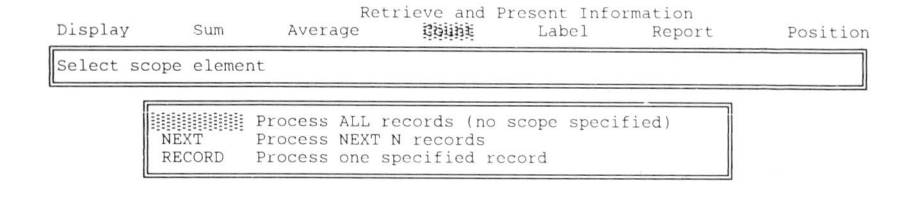

```
                        Retrieve and Present Information
Display      Sum       Average    Count      Label      Report         Position
Select scope element

              ::::::::: Process ALL records (no scope specified)
              NEXT      Process NEXT N records
              RECORD    Process one specified record
```

Command: Count

Figure 23-1

Press the down arrow key, then the right arrow key, then select **FOR** and press the RETURN key. Select AM_OWED, the >. Enter 625.00, press RETURN and then the right arrow key. dBASEIII will then display the message – **4 records**.

Repeat for the **Sum** and **Average** commands.

PART SEVEN

Queries

■ SECTION 24
Creating a query file

Query files can be very useful if you want to check your records each time that you use them. You might want to search for a specific value or code and to re-enter the same search condition every time is a very time consuming exercise. To save time we are able to create **Query** files with whatever search conditions that are required.

In previous sections we have created database files, now we must do the same with our Query file, create it and then save it.

When we need to use a Query file, we would use the Set Up menu, we are also able to create more than one Query file.

We will now create a Query file and use it. To do this first ensure that you are in the Assistant menu. Move the highlighted bar to the Set Up menu and select **Database file** and then select drive B. From the submenu of files available select CUSTACC.DBF and press the RETURN key, answer 'N' to the index prompt and press the RETURN key.

Now move to the **Create** menu and select **Query**, then drive B. dBASEIII Plus screen should then look as follows:

```
Set Up  Create  Update  Position  Retrieve  Organize Modify Tools    01:14:26 am
        Database file
        Format
        View
        Query
        Report
        Label

              Enter the name of the file:




Command: CREATE QUERY B:
ASSIST              <B:>OWED                    Rec: 1/11           Ins      Caps
```

Figure 24-1

■ SECTION 24
Creating a query file

At the prompt enter QUERY1 as the name of the file and press RETURN, the screen will then look as follows:

```
Set Filter              Nest           Display           Exit    01:15:24 am
┌─────────────────────────────────────────────────┐
│ Field Name                                      │
│ Operator                                        │
│ Constant/Expression                             │
│ Connect                                         │
│ ─────────────────────────────────────────────── │
│ Line Number         1                           │
└─────────────────────────────────────────────────┘
```

Line	Field	Operator	Constant/Expression	Connect
1				
2				
3				
4				
5				
6				
7				

CREATE QUERY   [<B:>[B:QUERY1.QRY   [Opt: 1/2   [Ins   [Caps

Figure 24-2

At the top of the screen the Query menu bar appears, the four menus and their submenus are as follows:

```
Set Filter              Nest           Display     Exit

Field Name              Add                        Save
Operator                  Start:0                  Abandon
Constant/Expression       End:   0
Connect                 Remove
                          Start:0
Line Number    1          End:   0
```

101

■ SECTION 24
Creating a query file

Now let's start creating our Query file.

Press RETURN to select the **Field Name**, then select DISCOUNT from the field submenu and press RETURN.

```
Set Filter          Nest         Display          Exit   01:17:14 am
┌─────────────────────────────────────────────────────────────────┐
│ Field Name         DISCOUNT                                     │
│ Operator                                                        │
│ Constant/Expression                                             │
│ Connect                                                         │
├─────────────────────────────────────────────────────────────────┤
│ Line Number        1                                            │
└─────────────────────────────────────────────────────────────────┘
```

Line	Field	Operator	Constant/Expression	Connect
1	DISCOUNT			
2				
3				
4				
5				
6				
7				

CREATE QUERY |<B:>|B:QUERY1.QRY |Opt: 2/5 |Ins | Caps

Figure 24-3

Discount has now appeared in the table at the bottom of the screen.

Now select **Operator** and press the RETURN key, another submenu will be shown on the screen. This one shows all the valid operators that may be used in dBASEIII Plus.

Now select >= **More than or equal** and press the RETURN key. The screen should look as in Figure 24-4.

■ SECTION 24
Creating a query file

```
Set Filter            Nest              Display         Exit  01:18:08 am
┌─────────────────────────────────────────────────────┐
│ Field Name         DISCOUNT                          │
│ Operator           More than or equal                │
│ Constant/Expression                                  │
│ Connect                                              │
│                                                      │
│ Line Number        1                                 │
└─────────────────────────────────────────────────────┘
```

Line	Field	Operator	Constant/Expression	Connect
1	DISCOUNT	More than or equal		
2				
3				
4				
5				
6				
7				

```
CREATE QUERY    <B:>B:QUERY1.QRY         Opt: 3/5              Ins    Caps
```

Figure 24–4

Next select **Constant/Expression** and enter the figure 6.00 at the prompt and press the RETURN key. We now have the first part of our conditional expression created:

```
        DISCOUNT More than or equal 6.00
```

appears in line one of our table.

Now select **Connect** and press RETURN, this brings up the submenu to link the first expression with the next one if required in our search condition. Select **Combine with** .OR. and press RETURN, the screen should look as Figure 24–5.

SECTION 24
Creating a query file

```
Set Filter         Nest          Display          Exit   01:19:04 am
┌─────────────────────────────────────────────────┐
│ Field Name                                      │
│ Operator                                        │
│ Constant/Expression                             │
│ Connect                                         │
├─────────────────────────────────────────────────┤
│ Line Number        2                            │
└─────────────────────────────────────────────────┘
```

Line	Field	Operator	Constant/Expression	Connect
1	DISCOUNT	More than or equal	6.00	.OR.
2				
3				
4				
5				
6				
7				

CREATE QUERY   <B:>[B:QUERY1.QRY   Opt: 1/2   Ins   Caps

Figure 24–5

We have now completed the first line of our table, the line number will now change to 2 with the menu completely clear and awaiting the input for the second search condition.

Now we will enter our second search condition from the AM_OWED field.

■ SECTION 24
Creating a query file

Firstly select AM_OWED for the **Field Name** from the submenu, then select <= **Less than or equal** for the Operator from its submenu. Now enter 625.00 against the prompt at **Constant/Expression**, then select **Connect** and then **Combine with** .AND., the screen should then look as follows:

```
Set Filter        Nest           Display           Exit    01:19:58 am
Field Name
Operator
Constant/Expression
Connect

Line Number         3
```

Line	Field	Operator	Constant/Expression	Connect
1	DISCOUNT	More than or equal	6.00	.OR.
2	AM_OWED	Less than or equal	625.00	.AND.
3				
4				
5				
6				
7				

```
CREATE QUERY     <B:>B:QUERY1.QRY            Opt: 1/2                Ins     Caps
```

Figure 24–6

Now enter the last condition:

```
Field Name             —   CRE_LMT
Operator               —   > More than
Constant/Expression    —   500.00
Connect                —   No combination
```

105

■ SECTION 24
Creating a query file

Now our finished Query table should look like this:

Set Filter	Nest	Display	Exit 01:20:50 am

Field Name	CRE_LIM
Operator	More than
Constant/Expression	500.00
Connect	

Line Number 3

Line	Field	Operator	Constant/Expression	Connect
1	DISCOUNT	More than or equal	6.00	.OR.
2	AM_OWED	Less than or equal	625.00	.AND.
3	CRE_LIM	More than	500.00	
4				
5				
6				
7				

CREATE QUERY |<B:>|B:QUERY1.QRY |Opt: 5/5 |Ins | Caps

Figure 24-7

Now press the right arrow key to exit the Set Filter mode and move on to the **Nest** menu.
When dBASEIII Plus evaluates an expression containing logical operators, these will be evaluated in the order:

.NOT., .AND., .OR.

In the case that we have just set up, we require dBASE to evaluate an .OR. before an .AND.

DISCOUNT => 6.00 OR AM_OWED <= 625.00 AND CRE_LMT > 500

To get over this problem we can **Nest** the expressions in parentheses, this will override the standard precedence .NOT., .AND., .OR. To do this we must put the parentheses around each statement in the order that we require it to be evaluated.

■ SECTION 24
Creating a query file

In our example the first expression that we require to be evaluated is:

(DISCOUNT => 6.00 or AM_OWED <= 625.00)

and the next expression is:

((DISCOUNT => 6.00 or AM_OWED <= 625.00) AND CRE_LMT > 500)

As usual make sure that each set of parentheses are closed. Now we have written it down let's use the **Nest** menu to enter our parentheses.

Select **Start** and against the prompt type '1' and press RETURN. A parentheses will be shown before the word DISCOUNT in line 1 of our table, now select **End** and type '2', another parentheses will appear in line 2 after 625.00. To finish our expression move the highlighted bar to **Start** and type '1' again, then **End** and type '3'. Our screen should now look like this:

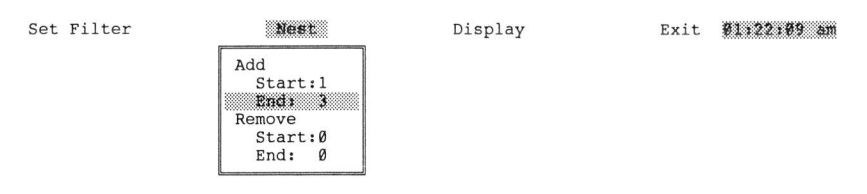

```
Set Filter          Nest            Display            Exit    01:22:09 am
                ┌──────────────┐
                │ Add          │
                │   Start:1    │
                │   End:   3   │
                │ Remove       │
                │   Start:0    │
                │   End:   0   │
                └──────────────┘
```

Line	Field	Operator	Constant/Expression	Connect
1	((DISCOUNT	More than or equal	6.00	) .OR.
2	AM_OWED	Less than or equal	625.00	) .AND.
3	CRE_LIM	More than	500.00	)
4				
5				
6				
7				

CREATE QUERY   <B:>B:QUERY1.QRY   Opt: 2/4   Ins   Caps

Figure 24-8

107

SECTION 24
Creating a query file

Now to see which records match the conditions that we have set, exit the **Nest** menu and select **Display** and then press the RETURN key. The first record will then be shown which satisfies the conditions that we set up in our Query file.

```
Set Filter            Nest              Display              Exit    #1:23:01 am
CUST_NO      C008
CUST_NAME    AMAD LTD
DISCOUNT     10.00
CRE_LIM      1000.00
AM_OWED         49.67
SPEND_TD     3241.46
SPEND_LY     9629.98
```

Line	Field	Operator	Constant/Expression	Connect
1	((DISCOUNT	More than or equal	6.00	.OR.
2	AM_OWED	Less than or equal	625.00	) .AND.
3	CRE_LIM	More than	500.00	)
4				
5				
6				
7				

CREATE QUERY |<B:>|B:QUERY1.QRY |Rec: 3/11 |Ins | Caps

Figure 24-9

Then if we use the **PgDn** key we can display any of the other records that match, in our database file these are:

```
C002  —  LUBRICAL LTD
C004  —  OKONI UK. LTD
C008  —  AMAD LTD
C011  —  SOLE GROUP
```

If the record is too long and all of it cannot be seen press the **F1** key and the table of conditions will be removed, press **F1** again and they will reappear.

Now select **Save** from the **Exit** menu and press the RETURN key, the Assistant menu will reappear when dBASE has saved the Query file.

■ SECTION 24
Creating a query file

If we want to use our new Query file when we first use dBASE, first select the Set Up menu, then **Database File** and then select the file that you wish to work on. Then move the highlighted bar to **Query,** select drive B and then select the file QUERY1.QRY.

Exit the menu and move the highlighted bar to the Update menu and select **Edit**, press RETURN and the screen should look as follows:

```
╔═══════════════════╦═══════════════════╦═══════════════════╦═══════════════════╗
║ CURSOR   <-- -->  ║           UP DOWN ║ DELETE            ║ Insert Mode: Ins  ║
║ Char:    ←   →    ║ Field:    ↑   ↓   ║ Char:       Del   ║ Exit/Save:  ˆEnd  ║
║ Word:   Home End  ║ Page:   PgUp PgDn ║ Field:      ˆY    ║ Abort:       Esc  ║
║                   ║ Help:     F1      ║ Record:     ˆU    ║ Memo:       ˆHome ║
╚═══════════════════╩═══════════════════╩═══════════════════╩═══════════════════╝
CUST_NO
CUST_NAME
DISCOUNT
CRE_LIM
AM_OWED
SPEND_TD
SPEND_LY
```

Figure 24-10

PART EIGHT

Reports

■ SECTION 25
Creating a report

dBASEIII Plus

In this section we will look at how to create reports from the data that we have stored in our database files.

We are only able to create a report from an existing database file.

Firstly ensure that you are in the dBASEIII Plus Assistant menu, then select the **Set Up** menu and then **Data base file** and then drive B. Now select the file CUSTOMER.DBF, answer 'Y' to the prompt and then select the index file NAME.NDX and press the RETURN key. The word **Master** is then shown to the right of the file name, press the right arrow key to then exit the menu.

Move the highlighted bar to the **Create** menu and select **Report**, then drive B and press the RETURN key. dBASEIII Plus will then prompt:

Enter the name of the file:

Enter CUSTLIST and press RETURN to enter the name of the report format file. The Create Report Screen will now be shown:

```
                    Groups      Columns         Locate       Exit
┌─────────────────────────────────────┐
│ Page width (positions)      80      │
│ Left margin                  8      │
│ Right margin                 0      │
│ Lines per page              58      │
│ Double space report         No      │
│ Page eject before printing  Yes     │
│ Page eject after printing   No      │
│ Plain page                  No      │
└─────────────────────────────────────┘


┌──────────────────┬──────────────────┬──────────────────────┬──────────────────────┐
│ CURSOR   <-- --> │ Delete char: Del │ Insert column:   ^N  │ Insert:       Ins    │
│ Char:    ←  →    │ Delete word: ^T  │ Report format:   F1  │ Zoom in:      ^PgDn  │
│ Word: Home End   │ Delete column:^U │ Abandon:        Esc  │ Zoom out:     ^PgUp  │
└──────────────────┴──────────────────┴──────────────────────┴──────────────────────┘
```

Figure 25–1

■ SECTION 25
Creating a report

Across the top of the Create Report Screen is shown a menu bar and each of these menus have submenus which are as follows:

Options Menu

Option	Description
Page title	— This allows up to four lines of text at the top of each report page to be printed.
Page width (positions)	— This will let you set the number of characters on a line. The default is 80 and you are allowed any width between 1 and 500 (size of paper allowing).
Left margin	— This will set the number of spaces from the far left edge of the page and the first printed character. The default is 8, but any number from 0 to the page width as defined.
Right margin	— This will set the number of spaces between the last character allowed on the line and the edge of the paper. The default is 0, any number from 0 to, but not including the defined page width. If the left margin has been set to a value which is greater than 0, then the value will be subtracted from the defined page width, and this will determine the maximum figure.
Lines per page	— This will set the maximum number of lines which can be printed out on each page. The default is 58 lines, but the range can be between 1 and 500 lines.
Double space report	— The default setting is single-spacing, but if double-spacing is required, the report will print a blank line between each record.
Page eject before printing	— This will advance the paper to the start of the next page before starting to print again. The default is Yes.
Page eject after printing	— After printing the last record a blank page will be advanced. The default is No.
Plain page	— This will allow page numbers and the system date to be printed. The title will be printed on the front page only. The default is No (Information prints).

113

■ SECTION 25
Creating a report

Groups Menu

Option		Description
Group on expression	—	This will group the records according to an index field or expression.
Group heading	—	This will label the group for printing.
Summary report only	—	This will allow the printing of only summary information on the number of records in the group. The default is a full report.
Page eject after group	—	This will print each group of records on a different page. The default is that the groups will print on the same page.
Sub-group on expression	—	This will create a sub-group using an index field or expression.
Sub-group heading	—	This will label the sub-group for printing.

Columns Menu

Option		Description
Contents	—	This requires the entry of the field description from the database file that is being used to create the report.
Heading	—	This will allow the entry of a new title of the contents of the original field that has been used in the Contents menu.
Width	—	This will show the total width of the field (if the heading is wider than the existing field, the wider width will be shown).
Decimal places	—	Shows how many decimal places are being used, it is also possible to alter the number of decimal places.
Total this column	—	This allows you to total the column or not total it.

Locate Menu

This menu shows all the fields that have been used in creating the report and can also be used for modifying the report.

Exit Menu

Options		Description
Save	—	This will save the completed report format to the specified drive.
Abandon	—	This will allow you to abandon the report format that has been created.

SECTION 25
Creating a report

dBASEIII

To create a report in dBASEIII is a very easy matter, first ensure that you are in the **Set Up Environment** screen and then select the **Use** command, followed by drive B. The database file CUSTOMER will be shown, select this and then answer 'Y' to the prompt 'Indexed Y/N?, the file names 'NAME.NDX' and 'PERCENT.NDX' will be shown on the screen, now select NAME.NDX and press the RETURN key.

In the **Set Up Environment** screen, select the command **Create Report** by moving the highlighted bar, the screen should now look as in the Figure below:

```
Command: Create
File in use: B:CUSTOMER.dbf  Current record #:    3    Size (records):    11

  Left:    Right:    Next:   (or ENTER)    Help: F1
                          Set Up Environment                         READY
Use         Set Drive     Create         Create Label        Create Report
Create a new Report form.  (R - Option letter)
```

```
                        CREATE REPORT
   CREATE  REPORT  allows  you to design and save a report  layout  for  the
   active  database  file.   Once the report layout is created,  the REPORT
   command is used to produce the actual report.
                     Command Format:   CREATE REPORT
```

```
Command: Create
```

Figure 25-2

115

■ SECTION 25
Creating a report

Press the down arrow key and then dBASEIII will then prompt:

Enter the name of the file:

Enter the name 'CUSTLIST' and press the RETURN key to enter the name of the report file. The screen should now look as follows:

```
CURSOR    <-- -->      UP    DOWN     DELETE         Insert Mode:  Ins
Char:              Field:              Char:   Del   Exit:         ^End
Word:  Home End    Page:  PgUp  PgDn   Field:  ^Y    Abort:        Esc
Pan:     ^   ^     Help:    F1         Column: ^U    Jump:         ^Home
```

                              Page heading:


```
            Page width (# chars):          80
            Left margin (# chars):          8
            Right margin (# chars):         0
            # lines/page:                  58
            Double space report? (Y/N):     N
```

Figure 25-3

■ SECTION 26
Report heading and columns

dBASEIII PLUS

Now let's give our report a Title, press the RETURN key when the highlighted bar is on **Page title** in the **Options** menu. A panel will appear on the right side of the screen now –

Type: **Customer File Report** and press RETURN

Type: **QQQ Company Limited** and press RETURN

Press RETURN, to miss out the third line.

Type: **Customer Mailing List** and press RETURN

The screen should now look as follows:

```
              Groups        Columns         Locate         Exit
░░░░░░░░░░░░░░░░░░░░░░░░░░░░░░░
Page title                 Customer
Page width (positions)     80
Left margin                8            ░░░░░░░░░░░░░░░░░░░░░░
Right margin               0            Customer File Report
Lines per page             58           QQQ Company Limited
Double space report        No
Page eject before printing Yes          Customer Mailing List
Page eject after printing  No
Plain page                 No


  CURSOR    <--  -->    Delete char:    Del    Insert column: ^N    Insert:    Ins
  Char:      ←    →     Delete word:    ^T     Report format: F1    Zoom in:   ^PgDn
  Word:    Home  End    Delete column:  ^U     Abandon:       Esc   Zoom out:  ^PgUp
```

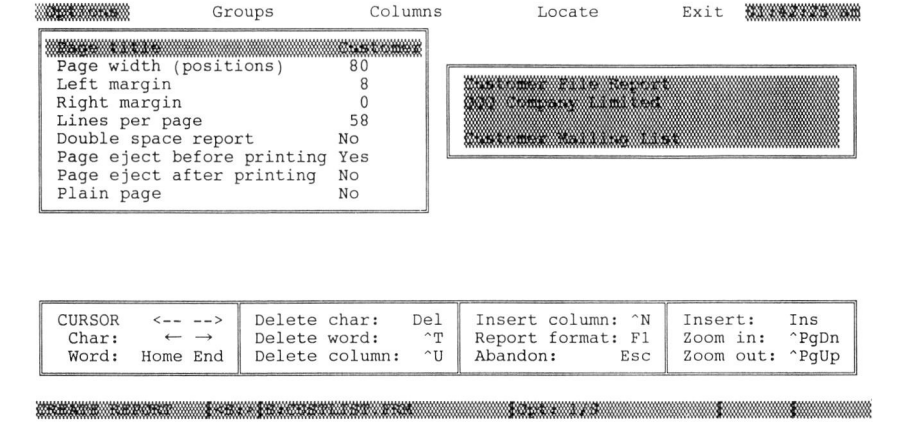

Figure 26–1

You can now specify the format of the page, i.e. page length, page width etc., refer to detailed description on the **Options** menu in section 25.

SECTION 26
Report heading and columns

If you do not wish to alter the page format, leave the **Options** menu by pressing the right arrow key and move to the **Group** menu, now select **Group or Expression** and press the RETURN key. Press **F10** and a submenu of all the fields in the database file CUSTOMER will be displayed to the left side of the screen as shown in Figure 26-2.

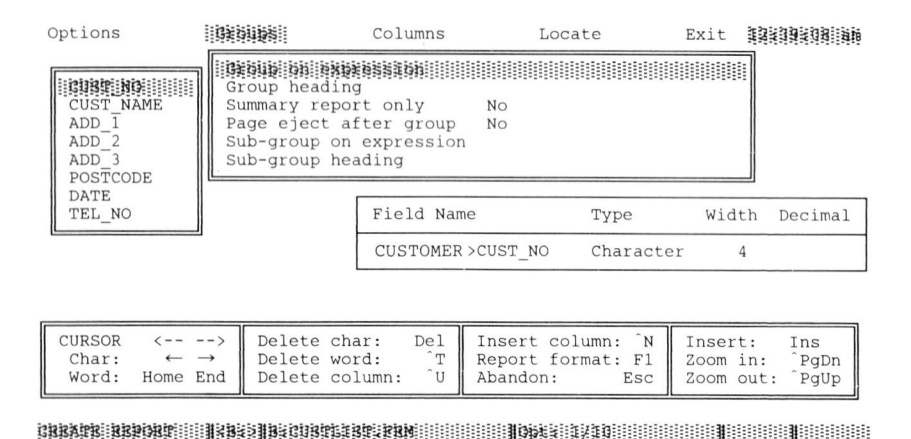

```
Options          Groups          Columns          Locate          Exit
                 Group on expression
 CUST_NO         Group heading
 CUST_NAME       Summary report only        No
 ADD_1           Page eject after group     No
 ADD_2           Sub-group on expression
 ADD_3           Sub-group heading
 POSTCODE
 DATE
 TEL_NO                          Field Name        Type        Width    Decimal
                                 CUSTOMER>CUST_NO  Character    4
```

```
 CURSOR     <-- -->      Delete char:    Del    Insert column: ^N    Insert:        Ins
 Char:      ←   →        Delete word:    ^T     Report format: F1    Zoom in:     ^PgDn
 Word:      Home End     Delete column:  ^U     Abandon:       Esc   Zoom out:    ^PgUp
```

Figure 26-2

Move the highlighted bar to CUST_NAME and press the RETURN key, press RETURN again and move the highlighted bar to **Group heading** press RETURN and then press **Ctrl-PgDn** and dBASEIII Plus will zoom into the text entry area as in Figure 26-3.

118

■ SECTION 26
Report heading and columns

```
Options              Columns         Locate       Exit
         Group on expression    CUST NAME
         Summary report only    No
         Page eject after group No
         Sub-group on expression
         Sub-group heading


CURSOR   <-- -->   Delete char:   Del   Insert column: ^N   Insert:   Ins
Char:    ←   →     Delete word:   ^T    Report format: F1   Zoom in:  ^PgDn
Word:    Home End  Delete column: ^U    Abandon:       Esc  Zoom out: ^PgUp
```

Figure 26–3

Type: **Customer Name** and press the RETURN key.

Now press the right arrow key to exit the menu and go to the **Columns** menu.

With the highlighted bar on **Contents** press the RETURN key and then the **F10** key, a submenu of the fields in the database file CUSTOMER will be shown on the right hand side of the screen. Place the highlighted bar on CUST_NO and press the RETURN key and then once more.

In the Report Format section of the screen 4 'X's are shown, this is the width of the field CUST_NO. Now move the highlighted bar to **Heading** and press the RETURN key, press it twice more and then enter:

> **Customer** and press RETURN.
>
> **Number** and press RETURN.

119

■ SECTION 26
Report heading and columns

The words Customer Number will be shown in the Report Format and the width will be shown as 8, as shown below:

```
Options         Groups          Columns         Locate          Exit    #1:36:27 am
                        Contents                CUST_NO
                        Heading                 ;;Customer;Number
                        Width                   8
                        Decimal places
                        Total this column
```

```
┌──Report Format──────────────────────────────────────────────────────┐
│>>>>>>>>   --------------------------------------------------------- │
│           Customer                                                  │
│           Number                                                    │
│    XXXX                                                             │
└─────────────────────────────────────────────────────────────────────┘
CREATE REPORT   |<B:>|B:CUSTLIST.FRM            |Column: 1       |Ins  |
```

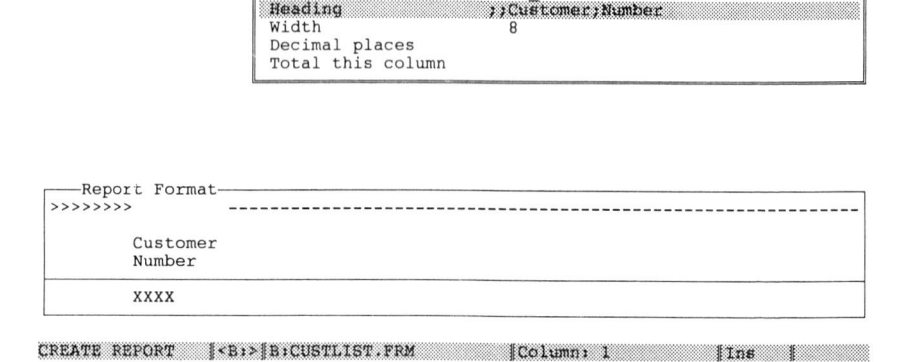

Figure 26–4

Now repeat the previous method and input the following information:

	Contents	Heading	Total this column
1.	ADD_3	Location	—
2.	DISCOUNT	Disc	No
3.	TEL_NO	Customer Telephone	—

When all the entries have been completed the screen should look as in Figure 26–5.

Now press the right arrow key and move the highlighted bar to the **Exit** menu and select **Save** and press the RETURN key. dBASE III Plus will now save the file CUSTLIST.FRM and return to the Assistant menu.

■ SECTION 26
Report heading and columns

```
Options        Groups       Columns        Locate      Exit   01:46:53 am
                          ┌─────────────────────────────────────────────┐
                          │ Contents         TEL_NO                     │
                          │ Heading          ;;Customer;Telephone       │
                          │ Width            12                         │
                          │ Decimal places                              │
                          │ Total this column                           │
                          └─────────────────────────────────────────────┘



   ┌─Report Format──────────────────────────────────────────────────────
   │>>>>                                                 ------------------
   │
   │   Customer                                     Customer
   │   Number    Location                      Disc Telephone
   │
   │   XXXX      XXXXXXXXXXXXXXXXXXXXXXXXX     ##.## XXXXXXXXXXX

CREATE REPORT   |<B:>|B:CUSTLIST.FRM             |Column: 4
```

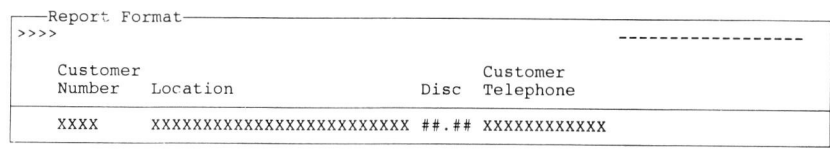

Figure 26-5

dBASEIII

Now we can enter a title to the **Page heading** screen. Press the space bar six times and then:

Type: **Customer File Report** and then press RETURN.

Press the space bar six times.

Type: **QQQ Company Limited** and press RETURN.

Press RETURN again, and then the space bar six times.

Type: **Customer Mailing List** and press the RETURN key.

The cursor will now move to the **Page width**(# **chars)**: prompt, press the RETURN key to remain the same. Type '**0**' against the **Left margin** prompt to alter the figure from 8, and then press the RETURN key four times to accept the default values to all the prompts. The screen should now look as follows:

121

■ SECTION 26
Report heading and columns

```
CURSOR    <-- -->            UP    DOWN      DELETE            Insert Mode:  Ins
Char:              Field:                    Char:  Del        Exit:         ^End
Word:     Home End Page:  PgUp  PgDn         Field:   ^Y       Abort:        Esc
Pan:       ^   ^   Help:        F1           Column:  ^U       Jump:         ^Home
```

Group/subtotal on:

Summary report only? (Y/N): N   Eject after each group/subtotal? (Y/N): N

Group/subtotal heading:

Subgroup/sub-subtotal on:

Subgroup/subsubtotal heading:

Figure 26-6

At present do not enter any information on this screen, but press the **PgDn** key to move onto the next screen of the report as shown below:

```
CURSOR    <-- -->            UP    DOWN      DELETE            Insert Mode:  Ins
Char:              Field:                    Char:  Del        Exit:         ^End
Word:     Home End Page:  PgUp  PgDn         Field:   ^Y       Abort:        Esc
Pan:       ^   ^   Help:        F1           Column:  ^U       Jump:         ^Home
```

                              Field 1   Columns left =   72
>>>>>>>>--

Field
  contents

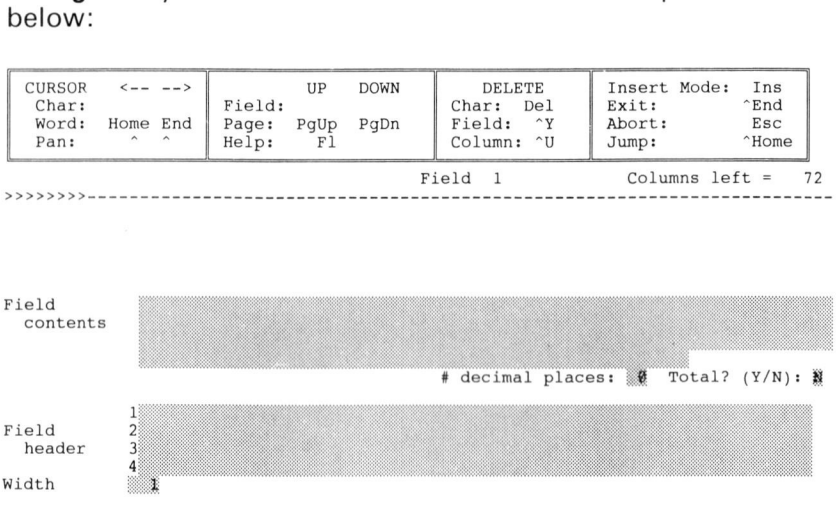

                                  # decimal places: @   Total? (Y/N): N
              1
Field   2
  header   3
              4
Width   1

Figure 26-7

122

■ SECTION 26
Report heading and columns

At the prompt enter the field name CUST_NO and press the RETURN key, the cursor will then move to line 1 of the **Field header** section of the screen:

Type: **Customer** on line 1 and then press the RETURN key.

Type: **Number** on line 2 and press RETURN.

The **Width** field should now be showing 8 at the bottom of the screen.

Now press the down arrow key until **Field 2** screen appears. Now repeat the same procedure, and enter the following:

	Field Contents	Field header	Total(Y/N)
Field 2:	ADD_3	Location	—
Field 3:	DISCOUNT	Disc.	N
Field 4:	TEL_NO	Customer Telephone	—

The screen will now look as follows:

```
CURSOR   <-- -->              UP    DOWN     DELETE          Insert Mode:  Ins
Char:     <   >      Field:                  Char:  Del      Exit:        ^End
Word:   Home End     Page:  PgUp   PgDn      Field:   ^Y     Abort:        Esc
Pan:     ^<  ^>      Help:    F1              Column:  ^U     Jump:       ^Home
```

                                    Field 5   Columns left =   20
Customer Location   Disc Customer Telephone --------------------

XXXX   XXXXXXXXXXXXXXXXXXXXXXXXX 99.99 XXXXXXXXXXXX
Field
    contents

                                    # decimal places: ▓ Total? (Y/N): ▓

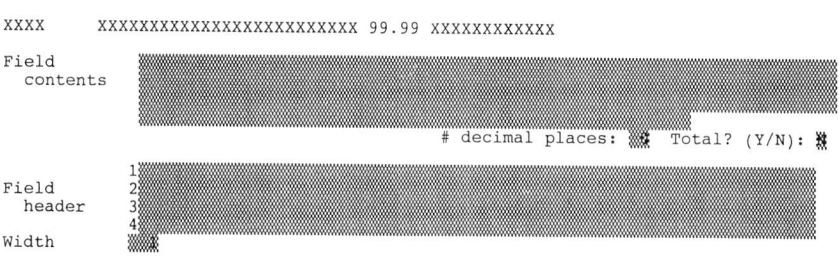

            1
Field   2
    header 3
            4
Width

Figure 26-8

To complete the report form just press the RETURN key again and dBASEIII will then save the report that you have just created.

■ SECTION 27
Modify an existing report

dBASEIII PLUS

To modify an existing report make sure that you are in the Assistant menu, then move the highlighted bar to the **Modify** menu and select **Report** from the menu and then press the RETURN key, select drive B, and then CUSTLIST.FRM and press RETURN. The original screen which showed the **Options** menu will be shown.

In this case we require an extra column of information on our report. Move the highlighted bar to the **Locate** menu and the screen should look as follows:

```
Options        Groups        Columns        Locate        Exit    #1:48:58 am
                                            CUST_NO
                                            ADD_3
                                            DISCOUNT
                                            TEL_NO




     ─Report Format─────────────────────────────────────────────────
     >>>>>>>>                                                  ────────────────
           Customer                              Customer
           Number   Location                Disc Telephone

             XXXX   XXXXXXXXXXXXXXXXXXXXXXX ##.## XXXXXXXXXXX

MODIFY REPORT   |<B:>|B:CUSTLIST.FRM          |Opt: 1/4
```

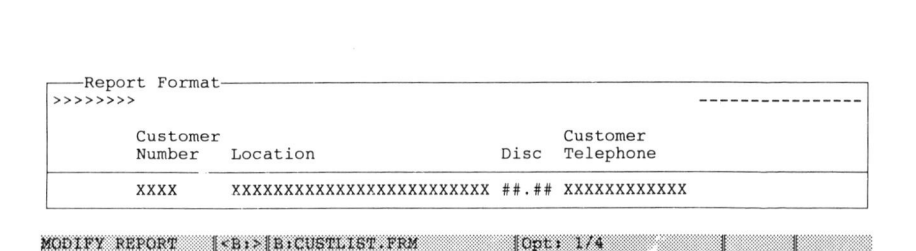

Figure 27–1

The submenu of the **Locate** menu is showing all the fields that we have used so far to create our report.

Move the highlighted bar down to the **DISCOUNT** field and press the RETURN key, the **Columns** menu will be shown, with all the information previously input, now press **Ctrl-N** and the screen should look as follows:

■ SECTION 27
Modify an existing report

```
Options        Groups        Columns           Locate         Exit    01:49:47 am
                             Contents
                             Heading
                             Width                     0
                             Decimal places
                             Total this column


        ┌─Report Format─────────────────────────────────────────────────────
        │>>>>>>>>                          ?                   ---------------
        │
        │       Customer                           Customer
        │       Number   Location             Disc Telephone
        │
        │       XXXX     XXXXXXXXXXXXXXXXXXXXXXX   ##.## XXXXXXXXXXX

MODIFY REPORT    |<B:>|B:CUSTLIST.FRM           |Column: 3           |        |
```

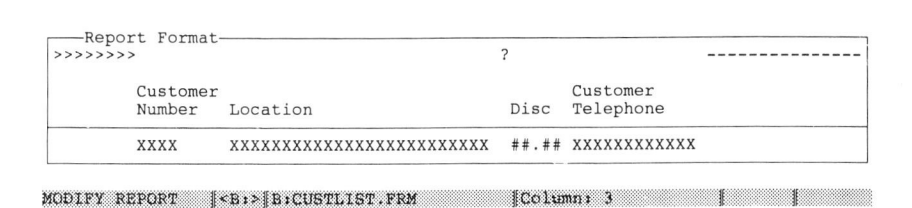

Figure 27–2

Pressing the **Ctrl-N** keys has inserted an extra column within our report.

Now enter the following details for the extra column:

```
Contents  —  Date
Heading   —  Date
```

The screen should now look as Figure 27–3.

To exit the menu press the right arrow key and move to the **Exit** menu and select **Save**, to save the modified report.

125

■ SECTION 27
Modify an existing report

```
Options        Groups        Columns         Locate        Exit    01:50:40 am
                       ┌────────────────────────────────────────────────────┐
                       │ Contents            DATE                           │
                       │ Heading             ;;;Date                        │
                       │ Width               8                              │
                       │ Decimal places                                     │
                       │ Total this column                                  │
                       └────────────────────────────────────────────────────┘




┌──Report Format───────────────────────────────────────────────────────────────┐
│ >>>>>>>>                                                              ------ │
│                                                                              │
│         Customer                                       Customer              │
│         Number    Location               Date    Disc  Telephone             │
│                                                                              │
│         XXXX      XXXXXXXXXXXXXXXXXXXXXXX mm/dd/yy ##.## XXXXXXXXXXXX         │
│                                                                              │
MODIFY REPORT   |<B:>|B:CUSTLIST.FRM            |Column: 3      |         |
```

Figure 27-3

dBASEIII

To modify an existing report in dBASEIII from the Assistant menu, select **Create Report**, press the right arrow key and then enter the name of the report that you want to modify, in our case enter CUSTLIST. dBASEIII will then display the **Page heading** screen, if any alterations are needed to the title use the editing keys which are shown at the top of the screen. Press **PgDn** four times to reach the screen showing **Field 3**, the cursor will be on **Field contents**, now press **Ctrl-N** and the screen should now look as follows:

■ SECTION 27
Modify an existing report

```
CURSOR    <-- -->            UP    DOWN       DELETE         Insert Mode:  Ins
Char:     ← →      Field:    ↑      ↓         Char:  Del     Exit:         ^End
Word:   Home End   Page:   PgUp   PgDn        Field:   ^Y    Abort:        Esc
Pan:      ^← ^→    Help:     F1                Column:  ^U   Jump:         ^Home
```

```
                                          Field   3            Columns left =   19
Customer  Location                   ?Disc  Customer Telephone ------------------
Number

XXXX      XXXXXXXXXXXXXXXXXXXXXXXXX  99.99  XXXXXXXXXXXX
Field
  contents


                                         # decimal places: ▓  Total? (Y/N): ▓

                    1
Field               2
  header            3
                    4
Width               ▓
```

Figure 27-4

Now you can enter the information for the new heading at Field 3:

Type: **DATE** at the cursor and press the RETURN key.

Type: **Date** and press RETURN.

Now press the **PgDn** key and the screen should look as in Figure 27-5.

■ SECTION 27
Modify an existing report

```
CURSOR    <-- -->              UP   DOWN     DELETE         Insert Mode:   Ins
  Char:    ←   →    Field:     ↑     ↓      Char:  Del      Exit:         ^End
  Word:  Home  End  Page:    PgUp  PgDn     Field:   ^Y     Abort:         Esc
  Pan:    ^← ^→     Help:      F1           Column:  ^U     Jump:        ^Home
```

                                      Field   4   Columns left =   11
Customer Location   Date   Disc   Customer Telephone ----------
Number

XXXX   XXXXXXXXXXXXXXXXXXXXXXX xx/xx/xx 99.99   XXXXXXXXXXXX
Field   DISCOUNT
  contents

                                           # decimal places: Total? (Y/N):

              1 Disc
Field   2
  header   3
              4
Width

Figure 27-5

The date field has been inserted between location and Disc. Now press the **Ctrl-W** keys to save the amended report.

■ SECTION 28
Displaying and printing reports

dBASEIII Plus

To either display a report on the screen or to print a report, first make sure that you have saved your report and that you are in the Assistant menu. Then move the highlighted bar to the **Retrieve** menu, select **Report** and then drive B, press RETURN and then select the file CUSTLIST.FRM. In our report we only require the companies that have a DISCOUNT that is greater than 9.00 per cent.

Move the highlighted bar to **Build a search condition** and press the RETURN key, then select the DISCOUNT field and move the highlighted bar to > **Greater than** and press the RETURN key.

Now enter the number 9.00 at the prompt and press the RETURN key and then once more. Move the highlighted bar to **Execute the command**, enter 'N' against the prompt if you want the output to the screen only or 'Y' if you require a print-out. The report should look as shown below:

```
      Page No.     1
      01/01/80
                              Customer File Report
                              QQ Company Limited

                              Customer Mailing List


      Customer                                       Customer
      Number    Location            Date       Disc  Telephone


      ** Customer Name JONES A.J.
         C001       WEST GLAMORGAN         12/30/87 10.00 0792 496421
      ** Subtotal **
                                                    10.00
      *** Total ***
                                                    10.00
```

Figure 28-1

129

SECTION 28
Displaying and printing reports

dBASEIII

Return to the **dBASEIII Assistant** menu and select **Retrieve** menu and then select **Report**, press the down arrow key and the select drive B and press the RETURN key. The file name CUSTLIST.FRM will be shown, press the RETURN key to select it. dBASEIII will then prompt:

Output to printer?(Y,N):

Enter 'N' and the screen will be as in Figure 28–2, press the right arrow key to select **Process ALL records (no scope specified)** and then select **FOR Every record that satisfies condition,** move to the next screen by pressing the RETURN key.

```
                      Retrieve and Present Information
Display      Sum       Average     Count      Label     Report      Position
Select scope element

              Process ALL records (no scope specified)
       NEXT   Process NEXT N records
       RECORD Process one specified record
```

```
Command: Report FORM CUSTLIST.FRM
File in use: B:CUSTOMER.dbf  Current record #:    1    Size (records):    11
Drive B:    Press  to move on to next selection item.
```

Figure 28–2

■ SECTION 28
Displaying and printing reports

A submenu of all the fields in the database file CUSTOMER.DBF will be shown on the screen, move the highlighted bar down to the DISCOUNT field and press the RETURN key. dBASEIII will then prompt you to select one of the following:

=	Equal to
<	Less than
>	Greater than
>=	Greater than or equal to
<=	Less than or equal to
<>	Not equal to

Figure 28-3

Move the highlighted bar to > and then enter the value 8.00 at the prompt and press RETURN, then press the right arrow key and the report should be shown on screen as shown below:

```
Page No.   1
02/27/88
                              Customer File Report
                              QQQ Company Limited
                              Customer Mailing List

Customer  Location           Date       Disc   Customer Telephone
C004      SURREY             08/08/85   8.50   01 541 49621
C001      WEST GLAMORGAN     12/30/87   10.00  0792 496421
C008      MIDDX.             04/09/86   10.00  01 751 4311
C010      LONDON             02/06/87   10.00  01 99349374
```

Figure 28-4

The report shows the four accounts which have a discount level higher than 8.00 per cent.

131

PART NINE

Labels

■ SECTION 29
Creating labels

dBASEIII Plus

First make sure that you are in the Assistant menu, move the highlighted bar to the **Set Up** menu and then select the CUSTOMER database file, answer 'Y' to the index prompt and select the file 'NAME.NDX', then exit the menu using the right arrow key.

Move the highlighted bar to the **Create** menu and then select **Label** from the submenu and then press the RETURN key, then drive B. Now type **Mail** at the prompt for the file name and then press the RETURN key, the screen should now look as follows:

```
                        Contents                    Exit

Label width:           35
Label height:           5
Left margin:            0
Lines between labels:   1
Spaces between labels:  0
Labels across page:     1




CURSOR:    <-- -->  | Delete char:  Del | Insert row:        ^N | Insert:       Ins
   Char:            | Delete word:  ^T  | Toggle menu:       F1 | Zoom in:    ^PgDn
   Word:  Home End  | Delete row:   ^U  | Abandon:          Esc | Zoom out:   ^PgUp
```

Figure 29–1

SECTION 29
Creating labels

Along the top of the screen there is a new menu bar, the first one that is open is the **Options** menu with its submenu. Descriptions of the various options are shown below:

Options Menu

Option	Description
Predefined size	This will allow you to set the size of the label that is to be used, to alter the size press the RETURN key. The range of labels is 3 2/20 × 11/12 to 4 × 1 7/16.
Label width	This is determined by the size of the label, the maximum number of characters that is allowed on a single line is 120.
Label height	This is also determined by the label size, but can be any number in the range of 1 to 16.
Left margin	This will set the number of characters from the left-hand side of the paper to the first printed character. The range is between 0 to 120.
Lines between labels	This is the vertical distance, in lines, between rows of labels. This command has a range of 0 to 16.
Spaces between labels	This is the horizontal distance in spaces between columns of labels. The range is between 0 to 120.
Labels across page	This will give the number of labels that will be printed on the same line across the page. It has a range of 1 to 5.

For the purpose of this exercise, we will select the **Predefined size** as shown on the screen, press the RETURN key with the highlighted bar on **Predefined size**.

135

■ SECTION 30
Label contents

dBASEIII Plus

Now that the label dimensions have been set, press the right arrow key and move the highlighted bar to the **Contents** menu. The screen should look as in Figure 30-1.

With the highlighted bar on **Label contents 1:** press the RETURN key and then the **F10** key, a submenu of the database file CUSTOMER will appear on the left side of the screen, move the highlighted bar to the CUST_NAME field and press the RETURN key and again to select it. Now move to **2:**, press RETURN again and then **F10**, select the field ADD_1, and then select the following:

```
Options                 Contents              Exit
            ┌──────────────────────────────────────┐
            │ Label contents 1:                    │
            │                2:                    │
            │                3:                    │
            │                4:                    │
            │                5:                    │
            └──────────────────────────────────────┘



┌─────────────────────┬──────────────────────┬──────────────────┬──────────────────────┐
│ CURSOR:   <-- -->   │ Delete char:  Del    │ Insert row:   ^N │ Insert:       Ins    │
│ Char:               │ Delete word:  ^T     │ Toggle menu:  F1 │ Zoom in:    ^PgDn    │
│ Word:   Home End    │ Delete row:   ^U     │ Abandon:     Esc │ Zoom out:   ^PgUp    │
└─────────────────────┴──────────────────────┴──────────────────┴──────────────────────┘
```

Figure 30-1

```
3:      ADD_2
4:      ADD_3
5:      POSTCODE
```

The screen should now look as in Figure 30-2.

Now leave the **Contents** menu and move the highlighted bar to the **Exit** menu and select **Save** to save the file MAIL.LBL.

■ SECTION 30
Label contents

```
Options                  CONTENTS                    Exit
                    Label contents 1:  CUST_NAME
                                   2:  ADD_1
                                   3:  ADD_2
                                   4:  ADD_3
                                   5:  POSTCODE
```

```
CURSOR:    <-- -->   Delete char: Del   Insert row:     ^N   Insert:        Ins
  Char:              Delete word: ^T    Toggle menu:    F1   Zoom in:    ^PgDn
  Word:   Home End   Delete row:  ^U    Abandon:       Esc   Zoom out:   ^PgUp
```

Figure 30-2

Now leave the **Contents** menu and move the highlighted bar to the **Exit** menu and then select **Save**, to save the Label file MAIL.LBL.

dBASEIII

Select the **Set Up** menu in the **dBASEIII Assistant** and then set the drive to B, select the database file CUSTOMER.DBF, answer 'Y' when asked if the file is indexed, and then select the indexed file NAME.

Move the highlighted bar to the **Create Label** and press the down arrow key. dBASEIII will then prompt:

Enter the name of the file:

■ SECTION 30
Label contents

Type: **MAIL** and then press the RETURN key. The screen should now look as in Figure 30–3.

```
CURSOR    <-- -->      UP    DOWN        DELETE        Insert Mode:  Ins
Char:     ← →       Field: ↑  ↓         Char:  Del     Exit:         ^End
Word:     Home End  Page: PgUp PgDn     Field: ^Y      Abort:        Esc
Pan:      ^← ^→     Help:    F1         Column: ^U     Menu:         ^Home
```

```
                        Label contents:
1    ▓▓▓ CUST_NAME ▓▓▓▓▓▓▓▓▓▓▓▓▓▓▓▓▓▓▓▓
2    ▓▓▓ ADD_1 ▓▓▓▓▓▓▓▓▓▓▓▓▓▓▓▓▓▓▓▓▓▓▓▓
3    ▓▓▓ ADD_2 ▓▓▓▓▓▓▓▓▓▓▓▓▓▓▓▓▓▓▓▓▓▓▓▓
4    ▓▓▓ TRIM(ADD_3)+" "+POSTCODE ▓▓▓▓▓▓
5    ▓▓▓ CUST_NO ▓▓▓▓▓▓▓▓▓▓▓▓▓▓▓▓▓▓▓▓▓▓
```

Figure 30–3

Remember that by pressing the **F1** key the top part of the screen can be changed to show the structure of the database file CUSTOMER.DBF.

The parameters shown on the screen can be changed to alter the appearance of the labels. On screen, the labels which are defined are 3.5 inches wide, 5 lines high, the left margin is shown as being zero, one line between labels, zero spaces between labels and one number label across. As most printers normally print 10 characters to the inch (CPI) across the page and 6 lines to the inch. Therefore if we need 2 labels across there will be plenty of room. Move the cursor down to the field **Number of labels across**: and type: 2. By altering the fields you will be able to alter the format of the labels in any way you wish.

When you have entered 2 the cursor will have moved to the **Remarks** field, you are able to add comments to this field for future reference. Any information shown in this field will not be displayed on screen or printed.

■ SECTION 30
Label contents

Type: **2 labels 3.5 wide** and press the RETURN key.

The **Label contents screen** will be shown, with the cursor in line one, press the space bar eight times and then:

Type: **CUST_NAME** and then press the RETURN key.

Press the space bar eight times.

Type: **ADD_1** and press the RETURN key.

Press the space bar eight times.

Type: **ADD_2** and press the RETURN key.

Press the space bar eight times.

Type: **TRIM(ADD_3)+" "+POSTCODE** and press the RETURN key.

Press the space bar eight times.

Type: **CUST_NO**

The screen should look as in Figure 30–4, now press the RETURN key to save the Label file.

On line four we typed:

   TRIM(ADD_3)+" "+POSTCODE

The **TRIM** function has been used to trim off any blank spaces that dBASEIII has added to the contents of a field, therefore if we had not used the **TRIM** function the line would be displayed as:

LONDON   W3 2AB

139

SECTION 30
Label contents

A:\>

CURSOR	<-- -->		UP	DOWN	DELETE		Insert Mode:	Ins
Char:	← →	Field:	↑	↓	Char: Del	Exit:		^End
Word:	Home End	Page:	PgUp	PgDn	Field: ^Y	Abort:		Esc
Pan:	^←^→	Help:	F1		Column: ^U	Menu:		^Home

```
                         Label contents:
1    CUST_NAME
2    ADD_1
3    ADD_2
4    TRIM(ADD_3)+" "+POSTCODE
5    CUST_NO
```

Figure 30–4

with the **TRIM** function used the line will look as follows:

LONDON W3 2AB

The +" "+ will put a space between the field ADD_3 and POSTCODE.

dBASEIII will now have returned to the **dBASEIII Assistant** menu.

■ SECTION 31
Modify an existing label

dBASEIII Plus

Return to the Assistant menu and move the highlighted bar to the **Modify** menu and then select **Label**, press RETURN, select drive B, then the file MAIL.LBL and press the RETURN key.

The **Options** screen will be displayed, now any item on the screen can be altered. For the purpose of this example change the **Predefined size:** to 3½ × 15/16 **by 3**, and the **Label width** to 25 from 35, the reason for doing this is because 3 labels at 35 characters wide will not fit on our screen display or our 80 column printer. The screen should now look as follows:

```
                         Contents                Exit
  Predefined size:       3 1/2 x 15/16 by 3

  Label width:           25
  Label height:          5
  Left margin:           0
  Lines between labels:  1
  Spaces between labels: 2
  Labels across page:    3




 CURSOR:    <--  -->  Delete char: Del  Insert row:        ^N   Insert:          Ins
    Char:               Delete word: ^T  Toggle menu:       F1   Zoom in:       ^PgDn
    Word:  Home End   Delete row:  ^U  Abandon:          Esc   Zoom out:      ^PgUp
```

Figure 31-1

Move the highlighted bar from the **Options** menu to the **Exit** menu and select **Save**. dBASEIII Plus will now save the amended Label file 'MAIL.LBL.'

141

■ SECTION 32
Displaying and printing labels

dBASEIII Plus

When you wish to either see the labels on screen or a print-out, move the highlighted bar to the **Retrieve** menu and then select **Label**, press the RETURN key and then select **Execute the command**, answer 'N' to the printer prompt. The screen display should now look as follows:

```
JONES A.J.              LUBRICAL LTD            COMCOL LTD
89 CITY ROAD            ELTHAM WORKS            AIMTREE ROAD
SWANSEA                 PRODHOE                 DOUGLAS
WEST GLAMORGAN          NORTHUMBERLAND          ISLE OF MAN
SA1 8RG                 NE40 9JP                IM56 4SD

OKONI UK. LTD           SAA LTD                 MANNS LIMITED
OKONI HOUSE             RAVEN STREET            MOOR LANE
KINGSTON UPON THAMES    KEELE                   WOKINGHAM
SURREY                  STAFFORDSHIRE           BERKSHIRE
KT41 9PS                SA42 2JA                RG13 9QR

XYZ SYSTEMS LTD         AMAD LTD                SCRIBE SYSTEMS
12 RAM ROAD             78 WILES ROAD           OLD MILL LANE
TOTNES                  FELTHAM                 RIVER WAY
DEVON                   MIDDX.                  OXFORD
TQ4 2ST                 TW11 3DE                OX4 9BY

K.B.A                   SOLE GROUP
3 NEWTON PLACE          AIR HOUSE
ACTON                   WILLIAM ROAD
LONDON                  CHELTENHAM
W3 2AB                  GT48 3FT
```

Figure 32–1

dBASEIII

To display records move the highlighted bar to the **Retrieve** menu and select **Label**, press the down arrow key and select drive B, then MAIL.LBL and press the RETURN key. Now say 'N' to the printer prompt and you will be prompted to **Select scope element** as shown below:

—	Process ALL records (no scope specified)
NEXT	Process NEXT N records
RECORD	Process one specified record

Figure 32–2

■ SECTION 32
Displaying and printing labels

Press the right arrow key to move on to the next selection, which is **Select conditional statement if desired**, this is shown in Figure 32–3. Then press the right arrow again to list the labels on screen.

```
   —         → Continue to next item →
   FOR       Every record that satisfies condition
   WHILE     Until a record no longer satisfies condition
```

Figure 32–3

PART TEN

Using the dot prompt

■ SECTION 33
Commands from the dot prompt

In this section we will look at dBASEIII and dBASEIII Plus at the same time, noting any differences that occur between the two.

We will create an employee record named WAGES and use the various commands that can be used from the dot prompt.

To create the database file WAGES using the dot prompt and entering commands, all you have to do is enter:

.**CREATE WAGES** — If using a single disk drive.

or if you are using another drive you are able to specify it by placing the drive letter in front of the file name:

.**CREATE B:WAGES** — The file will be stored on drive B.

When either command has been entered, the screen will look as in Figure 9–3. Now enter the following field information:

	Field Name	Type	Width	Dec
1.	L_NAME	Character	15	
2.	F_NAME	Character	10	
3.	DEPT	Character	10	
4.	WORKS_NO	Numeric	4	
5.	DATE	Date	8	
6.	ANNUAL_PAY	Numeric	8	2

Now save by pressing **Ctrl-End** keys. dBASE will then ask:

Input data records now? (Y/N)

answer 'Y' and enter the following data:

	Record 1	Record 2	Record 3	Record 4
L_NAME	Roberts	Jones	Matthews	Williams
F_NAME	Mark	Steven	Robin	John
DEPT	Works	Works	Sales	Admin
WORKS_NO	34	89	101	45
DATE	010986	120585	092186	052885
ANNUAL_PAY	7500.00	7900.00	11500.00	9250.00

and then save it.

Now that we have some data in our file WAGES.DBF let's check it to see that it is all there. To do this we could just type at the dot prompt:

.**DISPLAY ALL** or .**LIST ALL**

■ SECTION 33
Commands from the dot prompt

All the records and their data would be shown on the screen as shown below:

```
Record#  L_NAME     F_NAME    DEPT     WORKS_NO  DATE       ANNUAL_PAY
      1  Roberts    Mark      Works          34  01/09/86      7500.00
      2  Jones      Steven    Works          89  12/05/85      7900.00
      3  Matthews   Robin     Sales         101  09/21/86     11500.00
      4  Williams   John      Admin          45  05/28/85      9250.00
```

What if we only want to see some of the information and also in a different order, we could type:

.DISPLAY ALL F_NAME, L_NAME, ANNUAL_PAY

.LIST ALL F_NAME, L_NAME, ANNUAL_PAY

The screen display would look as follows:

```
Record#  F_NAME    L_NAME      ANNUAL_PAY
      1  Mark      Roberts        7500.00
      2  Steven    Jones          7900.00
      3  Robin     Matthews      11500.00
      4  John      Williams       9250.00
```

Using Append

To add records using the APPEND command we would type at the dot prompt:

.SET MENU ON

.APPEND

dBASE will then display a blank record screen at the end of the file ready for input of new data. Enter the following data to our new file:

```
              Record 5    Record 6    Record 7    Record 8
L_NAME        Kynch       Stevens     Robins      Hughes
F_NAME        John        David       Walter      Mike
DEPT          Admin       Works       Sales       Sales
WORKS_NO      104         23          105         55
DATE          050286      100585      062886      061285
ANNUAL_PAY    8250.00     7900.00     10250.00    9750.00
```

147

■ SECTION 33
Commands from the dot prompt

Now use the LIST ALL command again at the dot prompt, to check that all the additional records have been entered and saved. The screen should then look as shown in Figure 33–1.

```
Record#   L_NAME      F_NAME       DEPT      WORKS_NO  DATE       ANNUAL_PAY
     1    Roberts     Mark         Works           34  01/09/86      7500.00
     2    Jones       Steven       Works           89  12/05/85      7900.00
     3    Matthews    Robin        Sales          101  09/21/86     11500.00
     4    Williams    John         Admin           45  05/28/85      9250.00
     5    Kynch       John         Admin          104  05/02/86      8250.00
     6    Stevens     David        Works           23  10/05/85      7900.00
     7    Robins      Walter       Sales          105  02/28/86     10250.00
     8    Hughes      Mike         Sales           55  06/12/85      9750.00
```

Figure 33–1

To BROWSE the records enter at the dot prompt:

. BROWSE

Then press the RETURN key, if the menu at the top of the screen is required or not required type either of the following commands at the dot prompt before entering the BROWSE command.

.SET MENU ON or **SET MENU OFF**

When the BROWSE command is executed the screen will display the last record in the file which is record number 8:

```
L_NAME------6 F_NAME-----5 DEPT---3 WORKS_NO—DATE-----5 ANNUAL_PAY
Hughes         Mike        Sales         55  06/12/85      9750.00
```

To View the other records in the file press the up arrow key and the next record will be displayed. To exit the BROWSE command press the **CTRL–END** keys to return to a blank screen at the dot prompt.

Another way to look at or for specific records is by either using the GOTO or the LOCATE commands, if the GOTO command is used and we wanted to look at record number three, type at the dot prompt:

.GOTO 3

Then press the RETURN key and enter:

.DISPLAY

148

■ SECTION 33
Commands from the dot prompt

dBASE will then display the following information on record 3:

```
Record#  L_NAME     F_NAME   DEPT    WORKS_NO  DATE       ANNUAL_PAY
     3   Matthews   Robin    Sales        101  09/21/86     11500.00
```

If the LOCATE command is used and we required any record with the Christian name David, we type the following at the dot prompt:

.LOCATE FOR F_NAME = "David"

Press RETURN and dBASE will show which record or records meet the requirement:

Record = 6

This shows that record 6 has the required information, now type:

.DISPLAY

and record 6 will be displayed on the screen:

```
Record#  L_NAME     F_NAME   DEPT    WORKS_NO  DATE       ANNUAL_PAY
     6   Stevens    David    Works         23  10/05/85      7900.00
```

To edit record 6, type at the dot prompt:

.SET MENU ON
.EDIT

■ SECTION 33
Commands from the dot prompt

You will now be able to edit record 6, and the screen will look as shown in Figure 33–2 below:

```
CURSOR      <--  -->              UP    DOWN       DELETE          Insert Mode:  Ins
  Char:      ←    →     Field:    ↑      ↓         Char:   Del     Exit/Save:    ^End
  Word:     Home  End   Page:    PgUp   PgDn       Field:  ^Y      Abort:        Esc
                        Help:     F1               Record: ^U      Memo:         ^Home
```

```
L_NAME      Stevens
F_NAME      David
DEPT        Works
WORKS_NO    23
DATE        10/05/85
ANNUAL      7900.00
```

APPEND   <B:> WAGES   Rec: 6/8

Figure 33–2

If the WAGES file required to be indexed say on the Works number, type at the dot prompt:

.INDEX ON WORKS_NO TO NUMBERS

Numbers being the file name for the indexed file, when the RETURN key is pressed dBASE will display the following information:

.INDEX ON WORKS_NO TO NUMBERS
100% indexed   8 Records indexed

Now enter:

.DISPLAY ALL

SECTION 33
Commands from the dot prompt

and dBASE will display all the indexed records as shown below:

```
Record#   L_NAME      F_NAME      DEPT      WORKS_NO   DATE         ANNUAL_PAY
     6    Stevens     David       Works           23   10/05/85        7900.00
     1    Roberts     Mark        Works           34   01/09/86        7500.00
     4    Williams    John        Admin           45   05/28/85        9250.00
     8    Hughes      Mike        Sales           55   06/12/85        9750.00
     2    Jones       Steven      Works           89   12/05/85        7900.00
     3    Matthews    Robin       Sales          101   09/21/86       11500.00
     5    Kynch       John        Admin          104   05/02/86        8250.00
     7    Robins      Walter      Sales          105   02/28/86       10250.00
```

If an indexed file had been required on the ANNUAL_PAY field the command at the dot prompt would have been:

.INDEX ON ANNUAL_PAY TO SALARY

Salary being the indexed file name, the file when displayed would look as:

```
Record#   L_NAME      F_NAME      DEPT      WORKS_NO   DATE         ANNUAL_PAY
     1    Roberts     Mark        Works           34   01/09/86        7500.00
     2    Jones       Steven      Works           89   12/05/85        7900.00
     6    Stevens     David       Works           23   10/05/85        7900.00
     5    Kynch       John        Admin          104   05/02/86        8250.00
     4    Williams    John        Admin           45   05/28/85        9250.00
     8    Hughes      Mike        Sales           55   06/12/85        9750.00
     7    Robins      Walter      Sales          105   02/28/86       10250.00
     3    Matthews    Robin       Sales          101   09/21/86       11500.00
```

In both examples the fields have been indexed automatically from the lowest to the highest.

A SORT file can be created in which records will be arranged according to either the descending or ascending order of the specified fields.

If we required a descending sort on the ANNUAL_PAY field, type at the dot prompt:

.USE WAGES

The USE command selects the file on which to do the sort, then type:

.SORT TO PAY ON ANNUAL_PAY/D

Press the RETURN key and then type:

.USE PAY

■ SECTION 33
Commands from the dot prompt

The new .dbf file PAY is now called into use, to enable to see the sort, now type:

.LIST ALL

dBASE will then display the records in the sorted file PAY.DBF as shown below:

```
Record#  L_NAME     F_NAME    DEPT     WORKS_NO  DATE       ANNUAL_PAY
   1     Matthews   Robin     Sales       101    09/21/86    11500.00
   2     Robins     Walter    Sales       105    02/28/86    10250.00
   3     Hughes     Mike      Sales        55    06/12/85     9750.00
   4     Williams   John      Admin        45    05/28/85     9250.00
   5     Kynch      John      Admin       104    05/02/86     8250.00
   6     Jones      Steven    Works        89    12/05/85     7900.00
   7     Stevens    David     Works        23    10/05/85     7900.00
   8     Roberts    Mark      Works        34    01/09/86     7500.00
```

The ANNUAL_PAY field has been sorted into descending order.

These are just some of the commands that are used in dBASEIII and dBASEIII PLUS from the dot prompt, below in Figure 33–3 are shown some of the more used commands.

```
HELP       CREATE      USE        SET        MODIFY
LIST       DISPLAY     BROWSE     APPEND     EDIT
REPLACE    DELETE      PACK       SKIP       GOTO
LOCATE     CONTINUE    INDEX      SORT       SEEK
REPORT     LABEL       SUM        AVERAGE    COUNT
IMPORT     EXPORT      COPY TO
```

Figure 33–3

From the dot prompt it is possible to check the status of dBASE by typing at the dot prompt:

.DISPLAY STATUS

and the following screen display will be shown split into two separate screens:

Figures 33–4 to 33–11 apply to dBASEIII PLUS.

■ SECTION 33
Commands from the dot prompt

Currently Selected Database:
Select area 1, Database in Use: B:PAY.dbf   Alias: PAY

File search path:
Default disk drive: B:
Print destination: PRN:
Margin = 0
Current work area = 1

Press any key to continue ...

Figure 33-4

Press any key and the second screen will be displayed:

```
ALTERNATE  - OFF   DELETED    - OFF   FIXED      - OFF   SAFETY     - ON
BELL       - ON    DELIMITERS - OFF   HEADING    - ON    SCOREBOARD - ON
CARRY      - OFF   DEVICE     - SCRN  HELP       - ON    STATUS     - ON
CATALOG    - OFF   DOHISTORY  - OFF   HISTORY    - ON    STEP       - OFF
CENTURY    - OFF   ECHO       - OFF   INTENSITY  - ON    TALK       - ON
CONFIRM    - OFF   ESCAPE     - ON    MENU       - ON    TITLE      - ON
CONSOLE    - ON    EXACT      - OFF   PRINT      - OFF   UNIQUE     - OFF
DEBUG      - OFF   FIELDS     - OFF
```

Programmable function keys:
F2 − assist;
F3 − list;
F4 − dir;
F5 − display structure;
F6 − display status;
F7 − display memory;
F8 − display;
F9 − append;
F10 − edit;

Figure 33-5

When any of the function keys are depressed dBASE will immediately execute the command. It is also possible to program different commands to the function keys. Refer to the dBASE manual for further information. Also in Figure 33-5 dBASE informs us what SET commands are either ON or OFF.

■ SECTION 33
Commands from the dot prompt

To alter these, the SET menu has to be accessed, type at the dot prompt:

.SET

Press RETURN and dBASE will display the following screen, showing the various Options that are available with the SET command:

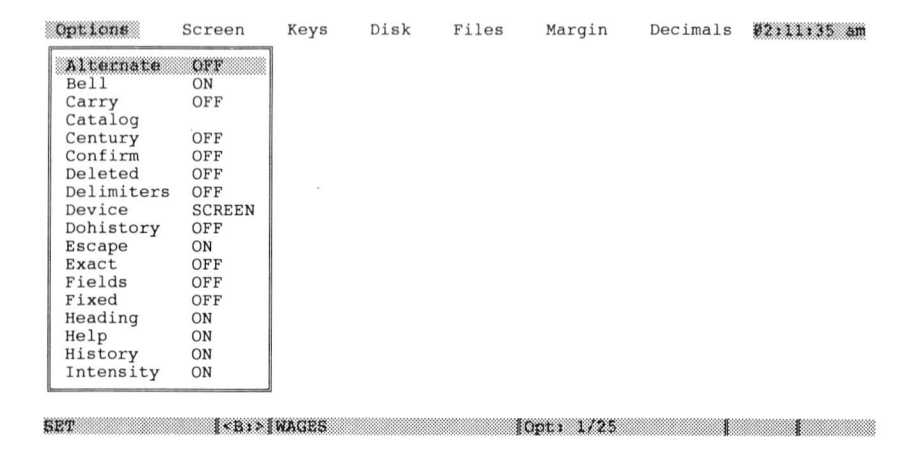

```
Options      Screen   Keys   Disk   Files   Margin   Decimals   #2:11:35 am
Alternate    OFF
Bell         ON
Carry        OFF
Catalog
Century      OFF
Confirm      OFF
Deleted      OFF
Delimiters   OFF
Device       SCREEN
Dohistory    OFF
Escape       ON
Exact        OFF
Fields       OFF
Fixed        OFF
Heading      ON
Help         ON
History      ON
Intensity    ON
```

SET   <B:>WAGES   Opt: 1/25

Figure 33-6

■ SECTION 33
Commands from the dot prompt

This screen shows a menu bar across the top of the screen, the submenus are as follows:

```
Display Type              Color
Standard Display
     Foreground:          White
     Background:          Black
     Intensity:           Dim
     Blink:               No
     Blank:               No
Enhanced Display
     Foreground:          Black
     Background:          White
     Intensity:           Dim
     Blink:               No
     Blank:               No
Border
     Color:               Black
     Intensity:           Dim
```

Figure 33-7

Keys

F2 assist;
F3 list;
F4 dir;
F5 display structure;
F6 display status;
F7 display memory;
F8 display;
F9 append;
F10 edit;

Figure 33-8

Disk

Default disk drive: B
disk drive search path

Figure 33-9

155

■ SECTION 33
Commands from the dot prompt

Files

Alternate
Format
Index

Figure 33-10

Margin

Left report margin: 00
memo field display width: 50

Decimals

Decimal places: 02

Figure 33-11

In dBASEIII the various screens would look as follows:

.DISPLAY STATUS

Currently selected database:
Select area   — 1, Database in use: b:pay.dbf   Alias — PAY

Press any key to continue ...

Figure 33-12

■ SECTION 33
Commands from the dot prompt

The screen will then scroll up when any key is pressed to show:

Press any key to continue ...

File search path
Default disk drive: B:

```
ALTERNATE  - OFF    DEBUG      - OFF   ESCAPE    - ON    MENU   - ON
BELL       - ON     DELETED    - OFF   EXACT     - OFF   PRINT  - OFF
CARRY      - OFF    DELIMITERS - OFF   HEADING   - ON    SAFETY - ON
CONFIRM    - OFF    DEVICE     - SCRN  HELP      - ON    STEP   - OFF
CONSOLE    - ON     ECHO       - OFF   INTENSITY - ON    TALK   - ON
UNIQUE     - OFF

Margin =     0
```

Function key F1 – help;
Function key F2 – assist;
Function key F3 – list;
Function key F4 – dir;
Function key F5 – display structure;
Function key F6 – display status;
Function key F7 – display memory;
Function key F8 – display;
Function key F9 – append;
Function key F10 – edit;

Figure 33–13

SECTION 33
Commands from the dot prompt

The SET menu in dBASEIII is as follows:

Options	Color	Keys	Disk	Files	Margin	Decimals

Enter SPACE BAR to switch an option ON or OFF

DEVICE	SCREEN
ALTERNATE	OFF
BELL	ON
CARRY	OFF
CONFIRM	OFF
DELETED	OFF
ESCAPE	ON
EXACT	OFF
HEADING	ON
HELP	ON
INTENSITY	ON
MENU	ON
PRINT	OFF
SAFETY	ON
TALK	ON
UNIQUE	OFF

Position with keys. ESC to QUIT. Enter SPACE to toggle function ON/OFF

Figure 33-14

The submenus of the other headings are:

Color

```
DISPLAY TYPE                    COLOR
STANDARD DISPLAY
    Foreground:                 White
    Background:                 Black
    Brightness:                 DIM
    Blinking:                   NO
ENHANCED DISPLAY
    Foreground:                 Black
    Background:                 White
    Brightness:                 DIM
    Blinking:                   NO
FRAME COLOR
    Color:                      Black
    Brightness:                 DIM
```

Figure 33-15

■ SECTION 33
Commands from the dot prompt

Keys

F1 help;
F2 assist;
F3 list;
F4 dir;
F5 display structure;
F6 display status;
F7 display memory;
F8 display;
F9 append;
F10 edit;

Figure 33-16

Disk

DEFAULT DISK DRIVE>   B
DISK DRIVE SEARCH PATH

Figure 33-17

Files

ALTERNATE
FORMAT
INDEX

Figure 33-18

Margin

LEFT REPORT MARGIN>   00

Figure 33-19

Decimals

DECIMAL PLACES>   02

Figure 33-20

Many of the commands that have been used in this section will be seen again in Part 12. This section shows an integrated program written using many of the commands that we have looked at.

PART ELEVEN

Commands

■ SECTION 34
Summary of dBASE III commands

!	Will display a field's contents in upper case.
	LIST !F_NAME
$	Substring function.
?	Displays the contents of a field, memory variable or the results of a mathematical equation.
??	Displays an expression line on the current line.
ACCEPT	This command will store a character string into a memory variable.
	ACCEPT <prompt> TO <memvar>
APPEND	Allows the addition of new data to database.
APPEND BLANK	Will add records to end of database file.
APPEND FROM	Will add records from other files to database files.
ASSIST	Calls up menu aids.
AVERAGE	Will compute the average of a numeric field.
BROWSE	This will display a screenful of records (up to 17).
CANCEL	Will abort program execution and return to dot prompt.
CHANGE	Edits specific fields or records in a database.
CLEAR	This will clear the screen.
CLEAR ALL	This will close all database, index, format and relational databases. Releases all memory variables and undoes all SELECT commands.
CLEAR GETS	This will release GET variables from the READ access.
CLEAR MEMORY	Will erase all current memory variables.
CLOSE	Will close a specified type of file.
CONTINUE	This is used with the LOCATE command to move to the next record meeting the specified condition.

■ SECTION 34
Summary of dBASE III commands

COPY FILE	This will duplicate any kind of file.
COPY TO	Will copy the contents of one database into another database.
COPY STRUCTURE	This will copy the structure of a database to another database without copying the contents.
	COPY STRUCTURE TO ADDRESS 2
COUNT	Counts the number of records in the active database.
CREATE	This will allow a database to be created and its structure to be defined.
CREATE LABEL	Will create a format file for mailing labels.
CREATE REPORT	Will create a custom report file.
DEFAULT	Will change the default drive for storing data files.
	SET DEFAULT TO C
DELETE	Marks a record for deletion.
	DELETE RECORD 12
DELIMITED	This copies dBASE databases to other data file formats.
	COPY TO REC.TXT DELIMITED WITH,
DIR	Displays the file directory:

    DIR   – Displays .DBF files.

    DIR *.*   – Displays all files.

    DIR *. NDX   – Displays all program files.

    DIR R*.PRG – Displays all .PRG files beginning with R.

    DIR ???.*   – Displays all file names that are three characters long.

■ SECTION 34
Summary of dBASE III commands

DISPLAY	This will show the contents of the data records.
	DISPLAY ALL
	DISPLAY CUST_NO,CUST_NAME,DATE
DISPLAY MEMORY	Displays current memory variables.
DISPLAY STATUS	Displays the current information about the active databases, index files, alternate files.
DISPLAY STRUCTURE	This will show the data structure of an active database.
DO	This will execute a program file.
	DO MENUPROG
DO CASE	This will allow the execution of only one of several paths, it must be terminated with the ENDCASE command.
DO WHILE	This sets up a loop in a program and be terminated with ENDDO.
EDIT	Displays a data record for editing.
	EDIT RECORD 23
EJECT	Sends a form feed to the printer.
ERASE	This will remove a specified file from the directory.
EXIT	Will exit from a DO loop without terminating the program.
FIND	This will search an indexed file for the first data record that matches the specified search key.
GO BOTTOM	Goes to the last record in a database.
GO TOP	Will start at the first record in a database.
HELP	Will call up help screens.
IF	Conditional branching command.
INDEX ON	This will create an index file of sorted data according to the contents of the specified key field.

164

■ SECTION 34
Summary of dBASE III commands

INPUT	This will display a prompt on screen and wait for a response.
	INPUT 'Stock Number:' TO STK_NO
INSERT	This will place a record into a specified position in the database file.
JOIN	Will create a new database file by merging the contents of two existing databases.
LABEL FORM	This will print labels using the specified label form file.
LIST	Shows the contents of a database.
LIST FOR	This will list data that will have some characteristic in common.
	LIST FOR CO_NAME = 'XYZ'
LOCATE	Positions the record pointer to a record with a specified characteristic.
LOOP	This will skip all the commands between it and the ENDDO command in a DO WHILE loop.
MEMORY	Displays memory variables in RAM.
	DISPLAY MEMORY
MODIFY COMMAND	This will call up the text editor to either create or edit a program file.
	MODIFY COMMAND MENUPROG
MODIFY LABEL	Create or edit a label file.
MODIFY REPORT	Create or edit a label file.
MODIFY STRUCTURE	Displays the current structure of the database.
NOTE	Starts the beginning of a remark line in a program.
	NOTE Enter Stock Code **INPUT 'Stock Code' TO ST_CODE**

SECTION 34
Summary of dBASE III commands

PACK — This will permanently remove records that have been marked for deletion.

PICTURE — This is used with the GET command to make templates and also define acceptable character types.

    @ 15,9 SAY 'PHONE NUMBER' GET PHONE PICTURE '(999)999-99999'

PARAMETERS — Will specify memory variables that use information passed by the DO ... WITH command.

PRIVATE — Hides memory variables in a program module.

PUBLIC — Makes memory variables global.

QUIT — This will exit dBASEIII back to the operating system's **A**> prompt.

READ — This is used with @, SAY and GET to read in field and memory variable data from the screen since the last CLEAR GET was issued.

RECALL — This will recover a record or records marked for deletion.

    RECALL RECORD 7

    RECALL ALL

REINDEX — Will rebuild all active index files.

RELEASE — Will delete all or selected current memory variables.

RENAME — Will change the name of a disk file.

    RENAME AAA.DBF TO ZZZ.DBF

REPLACE — This will change the contents of specified fields in an active database.

    REPLACE ALL WEEK_PAY WITH WEEK_PAY*1.28

    REPLACE ALL L_NAME WITH 'Roberts' FOR L_NAME = 'ROBERTS'

■ SECTION 34
Summary of dBASE III commands

REPORT FORM	This will display data from an active database file in report format.
	REPORT FORM STOCK
	REPORT FORM STOCK TO PRINT
RESTORE FROM	Will retrieve sets of saved memory variables.
RETURN	This will return control from a command file to the dot prompt or another command file.
RUN	Will execute a program outside of dBASEIII.
	RUN WS (This will run WordStar)
SAVE TO	Stores a copy of current memory variables to a memory file.
SEEK	This will search an indexed database file for the first record that matches the specified expression.
SELECT	Will place a database file in a specified work area, numbered 1 through to 10, or lettered A through to J.
	SELECT 1
	SELECT A
SET	Sets dBASEIII control parameters.
SET ALTERNATE TO	Creates a file for saving output.
SET ALTERNATE ON/off	Sends DOES NOT SEND output to a file.
SET BELL ON/off	This will determine if the bell sounds or not when a field is filled on an APPEND, EDIT, or custom screen.
SET CARRY on/OFF	Write DOES NOT WRITE contents of the last record into the APPEND record.

■ SECTION 34
Summary of dBASE III commands

SET COLOR ON/OFF   Sets the output display to colour/monochrome.

SET COLOR TO   Sets the screen display attributes.

The available colors and their codes are:

Color		Letter
Black	–	N
White	–	W
Blue	–	B
Brown	–	GR
Green	–	G
Magenta	–	RB
Cyan	–	BG
Red	–	R
Blank	–	X
Yellow	–	GR+
Gray	–	N+

An asterisk will indicate blinking characters.

A plus sign (+) will indicate high intensity.

SET COLOR TO B+,W

Sets display to high intensity Blue with a White border.

SET CONFIRM on/OFF   Will determine whether the pressing of the RETURN key is needed after filling a screen prompt.

SET CONSOLE ON/off   Will turn the video display on/off.

SET DEBUG on/OFF   This will send output of an ECHO to the printer when on.

SET DECIMAL TO   Sets the number of decimal places displayed.

SET DEFAULT TO   Specifies the default disk drive used when looking for disk files.

SET DELETED on/OFF   Sets whether data records marked for deletion are to be ignored.

■ SECTION 34
Summary of dBASE III commands

SET DELIMITER TO	This will specify characters for marking a field.
SET DELIMITER on/OFF	This will display full-screen fields delimited in normal video/IN REVERSE VIDEO.
SET DEVICE TO SCREEN /print	This will select the display medium, either to, SCREEN/printer.
SET ECHO on/OFF	Displays each line of a program file as it is being processed.
SET ESCAPE ON/off	This will determine whether a command file terminates when the Esc key is pressed.
SET EXACT ON/off	This will determine how dBASEIII compares either with an exact match or with the first two letters, i.e. With EXACT OFF, Roberts would match Robertson.
SET FILTER TO	Will cause a database file to limit the display of those records which match a set criteria, i.e.

SET FILTER TO F_NAME = "JOHN"

This will limit the output of LIST, LABEL, REPORT etc. to JOHNs.

SET FIXED on/OFF	This will set the number of decimal places that will be displayed in all numeric displays, and is usually used in conjunction with SET DECIMALS.
SET FORMAT TO	This will open a format file for data entry.
SET FUNCTION TO	This will reprogram the function keys (F1 to F10) to perform a specific task.

SET FUNCTION 8 TO 'DISPLAY'

SET HEADING on/OFF	This will set function key F8 to DISPLAY. Field names will or not be displayed above data in DISPLAY, LIST, SUM and AVERAGE commands.
SET HELP ON/off	This will determine whether or not dBASEIII will display the message 'Do you want some help?' when an error is encountered.

169

■ SECTION 34
Summary of dBASE III commands

SET INDEX TO	Will open the named index files.
SET INTENSITY ON/off	Will determine whether or not data fields will be displayed in reverse video on the screen.
SET MARGIN TO	This will adjust the left-hand margin for all printed output.
	SET MARGIN TO 12
	This will set the margin to 12.
SET MENUS ON/off	This will determine whether a menu is displayed during full-screen operations.
SET PATH TO	This will specify the search directory path.
SET PRINT on/OFF	Allows displays to be output to the screen or printer.
SET PROCEDURE TO	Used in advanced programming, subprograms are combined into a single file and then assigned procedure names.
SET RELATION TO	This links two databases based upon a field that they both have in common.
SET SAFETY ON/off	This will display a warning message when overwriting an existing file.
SET STEP on/OFF	This will cause the execution of a command file to pause after each command.
SET TALK ON/off	Allows dBASEIII to display a response to various commands or not during execution.
SET UNIQUE on/OFF	This will be used with the INDEX command to display an ordered listing.
SKIP	This will move the record pointer either forward or backwards through the records in the active database file.
SORT	This will rearrange records in a database file into a sorted order on one or more key fields in ascending or descending order.
STORE	This will store a value to a memory variable.

■ SECTION 34
Summary of dBASE III commands

SUM	This will add a column of fields, and display the total.
TEXT	This will display a block of text on the screen or printer. TEXT must be terminated with ENDTEXT.
TOTAL	This will sum the numeric values of an active database on a specified field, and will store the result to another file.
	TOTAL ON STOCK_CD TO TOTSTOCK
TYPE	This will display the contents of a disk file, either to the screen or the printer.
	TYPE MENU.PRG
	TYPE MENU.PRG TO PRINT
UPDATE	Will use records in one database to update records in another file.
USE	This will open an existing database file.
	USE CUSTOMER
WAIT	This will cause the execution of a program to pause until a key is pressed.
	WAIT "Do you wish to continue (Y/N)?" TO CONTINUE
ZAP	This will remove all the data records from a database file, but will not delete the structure of the file.

171

■ SECTION 35
Extra commands used in dBASE III Plus

CALL This will allow you to call binary file program modules that are loaded in memory from within a dBASEIII Plus program file.

CLEAR TYPEAHEAD This will empty the type-ahead buffer.

COPY STRUCTURE EXTENDED This will create a new database file with the four fields:

FIELD_NAME, FIELD_TYPE, FIELD_LEN, FIELD_DEC

CREATE QUERY This will create a new query file.

CREATE SCREEN This will create a new screen file.

CREATE VIEW This will create a new view file.

DISPLAY HISTORY This will output a list, either to screen or printer, of the commands that have been executed, and are stored in the history buffer.

EXPORT TO This will convert a dBASEIII Plus file to a PFS file.

IMPORT FROM This will convert a PFS file to a dBASEIII Plus file.

LIST HISTORY This will output a list of the commands that have been executed and are stored in the history buffer. It will scroll up the screen without pausing at each full screen display.

LOAD This enables you to load binary program files in memory and run them from memory with the CALL command.

MODIFY QUERY This will edit or create a query file.

MODIFY SCREEN This will edit or create a screen file.

MODIFY VIEW This will edit or create a view file.

■ SECTION 35
Extra commands used in dBASE III Plus

RESUME This will resume the execution of a program or procedure when it has been stopped by the SUSPEND command.

SET CATALOG ON/off This will add files to an open catalog.

SET CATALOG TO This will create, and opens and closes a catalog file.

SET DATE This will specify the format for the date expressions.

SET DATE BRITISH	–	dd/mm/yy
SET DATE AMERICAN	–	mm/dd/yy
SET DATE FRENCH	–	dd/mm/yy
SET DATE GERMAN	–	dd.mm.yy
SET DATE ITALIAN	–	dd–mm–yy
SET DATE ANSI	–	yy.mm.dd

SET DOHISTORY on/OFF This will determine whether or not commands from command files will be recorded in the history buffer as they are executed.

SET FIELDS TO This will select specified fields to be displayed.

SET FIELDS TO CUST_NO,TEL_NO,DISCOUNT

This will allow the three fields to be displayed.

SET HISTORY ON/off This will turn the history feature on or off.

SET HISTORY TO This will specify the number of executed commands that are to be stored in the history buffer.

SET HISTORY TO 9

The default number of commands stored is 20 and the range allowed is between zero and 16,000.

173

■ SECTION 35
Extra commands used in dBASE III Plus

SET MEMO TO   This will adjust the width of a memo field output.

SET MEMOWIDTH TO 45

The default width is 50 and the minimum number is 8 characters.

SET ODOMETER TO   This will define the update interval of the record counter for all commands which display a record count.

SET ODOMETER TO 12

SET ORDER TO   This will set up the open index file as the master file, or will remove control from all the open index files, without reopening the files.

SET ORDER TO [X]

Where [X] is an integer between 0 and 7, depending on the number of open index files.

SET SCOREBOARD ON/off   This will determine if dBASEIII Plus messages will appear on line 0 if SET STATUS is OFF.

SET STATUS ON/off   This will determine whether the status bar at the bottom of the screen is displayed or not.

PART TWELVE

An integrated program

SECTION 36
Main menu

Now we have looked at the sections on programming dBASE from the dot prompt, dBASE commands and functions, let's look at an Integrated Program using a series of menus to integrate the various programs. This section will deal with a customer file and a stock file all called from a main menu.

The menu that we require is shown in Figure 36–1 and the program is shown in Figure 36–2.

To start entering the program from the dot prompt first enter the following:

.MODIFY COMMAND MAINMENU

Then press the RETURN key and dBASE will then display it's word processor, now enter the program as in Figure 36–2.

```
************************************
******** M A I N   M E N U ********
************************************

     Option No.          Option

     1              Customer Menu

     2              Stock Menu

     3              Print Menu

     4              Quit

     Enter Option Number :
```

Command |<B:>|CUSTOMER |Rec: 1/11 | |

Figure 36–1

176

■ SECTION 36
Main menu

```
******************** MAINMENU.PRG ********************
SET TALK OFF
SET ECHO OFF
STORE " " TO CHOICE
DO WHILE .T.
     CLEAR
     ?"                         ****************************************"
     ?"                         ********  M A I N     M E N U ********"
     ?"                         ****************************************"
     ?
     ?
     ?"                         Option No.              Option"
     ?
     ?"                         1                       Customer Menu"
     ?
     ?"                         2                       Stock Menu"
     ?
     ?"                         3                       Print Menu"
     ?
     ?"                         4                       Quit"
     ?
     WAIT "                     Enter Option Number: " TO CHOICE
     DO CASE
          CASE CHOICE = "1"
               DO EDCUST
          CASE CHOICE = "2"
               DO EDPART
          CASE CHOICE = "3"
               DO PRMENU
          CASE CHOICE = "4"
               RETURN
          OTHERWISE
               LOOP
     ENDCASE
ENDDO
```

Figure 36-2 The main menu program.

To save the program press the **Ctrl-W** keys and dBASE will RETURN to the dot prompt. dBASE will automatically save the program as **MAINMENU.PRG** the **.PRG** extension being added by dBASE.

To run the program MAINMENU.PRG from the dot prompt enter:

.DO MAINMENU

The screen will then look as in Figure 36–1, showing the various sections that can be accessed from the menu

If '1' was pressed to get option one, the customer menu would then be displayed on the screen, as shown below in Figure 36–3.

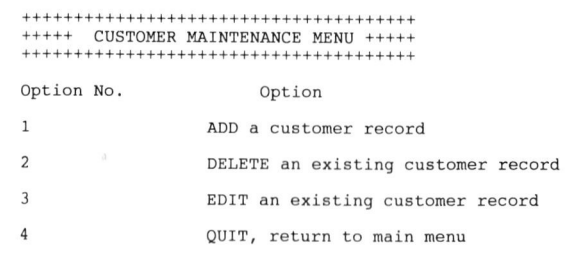

■ SECTION 37
Customer maintenance menu

```
+++++++++++++++++++++++++++++++++++++++++
+++++   CUSTOMER MAINTENANCE MENU   +++++
+++++++++++++++++++++++++++++++++++++++++
Option No.           Option

1                    ADD a customer record

2                    DELETE an existing customer record

3                    EDIT an existing customer record

4                    QUIT, return to main menu

        Enter Option Number :


Command      |<B:>|CUSTOMER              |Rec: 1/11 -          |          |
```

Figure 37-1

This submenu shows that we are able to perform various tasks with our customer records, these are:

Add a new customer record.

Delete an existing customer record.

Edit an existing customer record.

Quit this menu and return to the main menu.

The program to display this menu is shown in Figure 37-2, and can be typed in from the dot prompt as below:

.MODIFY COMMAND ADDCUST

SECTION 37
Customer maintenance menu

Press the RETURN key and enter the listing in Figure 37–2 below.

```
******************* EDCUST.PRG *********************
SET TALK OFF
SET ECHO OFF
STORE " " TO CHOICE
DO WHILE .T.
    CLEAR
    ?
    ?
    ?"              +++++++++++++++++++++++++++++++++++"
    ?"              +++++   CUSTOMER MAINTENANCE MENU +++++"
    ?"              +++++++++++++++++++++++++++++++++++"
    ?
    ?"              Option No.      Option"
    ?
    ?"              1               ADD a customer record"
    ?
    ?"              2               DELETE an existing customer record"
    ?
    ?"              3               EDIT an existing customer record"
    ?
    ?"              4               QUIT, return to main menu"
    ?
    ?
    WAIT"          Enter Option Number : " TO CHOICE
    DO CASE
        CASE CHOICE = "1"
            DO ADDCUST
        CASE CHOICE = "2"
            DO DELCUST
        CASE CHOICE = "3"
            DO EDITCUST
        CASE CHOICE = "4"
            RETURN
    ENDCASE
ENDDO
RETURN
```

Figure 37–2 The Customer Maintenance menu

This program will run automatically when option 1 is selected from the main menu:

CASE CHOICE = "1"

DO EDCUST

179

SECTION 37
Customer maintenance menu

If '1' was pressed again to select option one the screen would look as displayed in Figure 37–3.

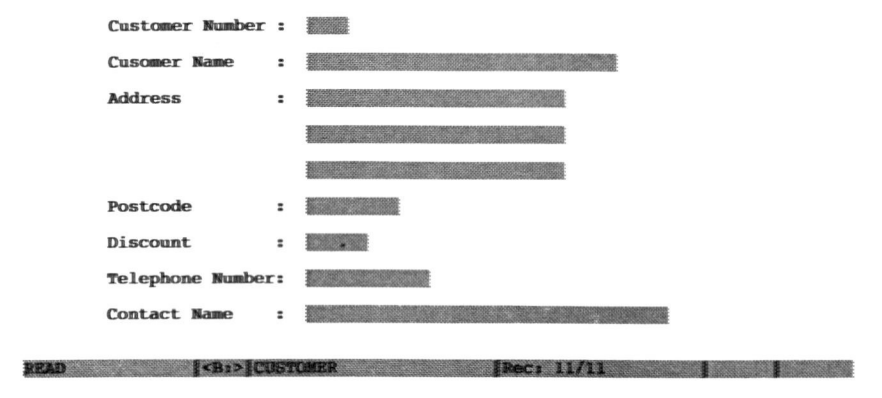

```
Customer Number :  ▓▓
Cusomer Name     :  ▓▓▓▓▓▓▓▓▓▓▓▓▓▓▓▓▓▓▓▓
Address          :  ▓▓▓▓▓▓▓▓▓▓▓▓▓▓▓▓▓▓▓▓
                    ▓▓▓▓▓▓▓▓▓▓▓▓▓▓▓▓▓▓▓▓
                    ▓▓▓▓▓▓▓▓▓▓▓▓▓▓▓▓▓▓▓▓
Postcode         :  ▓▓▓▓▓
Discount         :  ▓▓.▓
Telephone Number:   ▓▓▓▓▓▓▓▓
Contact Name     :  ▓▓▓▓▓▓▓▓▓▓▓▓▓▓▓▓▓▓▓▓
READ       <B:> CUSTOMER        Rec: 11/11
```

Figure 37–3

To type this program enter at the dot prompt:

.MODIFY COMMAND ADDCUST

Press the RETURN key and enter the following:

```
********************* ADDCUST.PRG *********************
SET TALK OFF
SET ECHO OFF
USE CUSTOMER
* Use custom format CUSTOMER.FMT
SET FORMAT TO CUSTOMER.FMT
APPEND BLANK
READ
RETURN
```

Figure 37–4 The adding a customer program

180

■ SECTION 37
Customer maintenance menu

This program uses the command:

USE CUSTOMER

Customer is the database file which must be CREATED before the mainmenu program is run. The details of the file CUSTOMER.dbf are as follows:

```
Structure for database: B:CUSTOMER.dbf
Number of data records:      4
Date of last update    : 04/03/88
Field  Field name_ type       Width      Dec
    1  CUSTNUMBER_ character      4
    2  CLIENTNAME_ character     30
    3  ADD1 _      Character     25
    4  ADD2  _     Character     25
    5  ADD3  _     Character     25
    6  POST_CODE   Character      9
    7  DISC   _    Numeric        6        2
    8  TEL_NO      Character     12
    9  CONTACT_    Character     35
** Total **             _       172
```

To do this from the dot prompt, type:

. CREATE CUSTOMER

Then press the RETURN key and then enter the information shown above.

The program ADDCUST also uses the program line:

SET FORMAT TO CUSTOMER.FMT

This line is calling up the program CUSTOMER.FMT, which enables dBASE to display as shown in Figure 37–3.

To enter the program CUSTOMER.FMT enter:

.MODIFY COMMAND CUSTOMER.FMT

■ SECTION 37
Customer maintenance menu

Press the RETURN key and then type the program as shown in Figure 37–5. It is important to remember that when creating a format file to type in the extension '.FMT' after the filename when using the MODIFY COMMAND, because if it is not typed in dBASE will automatically assign the extension '.PRG', making it a program file not a format file.

The program will enter information into the .dbf database CUSTOMER at its next record, by using the command APPEND BLANK in the ADDCUST program.

```
********************* CUSTOMER.FMT **********************
@3,8   SAY "Customer Number  : " GET CUSTNUMBER
@5,8   SAY "Customer Name    : " GET CLIENTNAME
@7,8   SAY "Address          : " GET ADD1
@9,8   SAY "                   " GET ADD2
@11,8  SAY "                   " GET ADD3
@13,8  SAY "Postcode         : " GET POST_CODE
@15,8  SAY "Discount         : " GET DISC
@17,8  SAY "Telephone Number : " GET TEL_NO
@19,8  SAY "Contact Name     : " GET CONTACT
```

Figure 37–5 The Customer Format program

If the number two key is pressed when the Customer Maintenance Menu is displayed, option 2 will be selected.

This option will enable you to delete a customer from the existing customer records. Before it is possible to delete a customer record it must be found first, therefore at this point we need to write two programs, one to delete and the other to find the customer.

When option two is selected the screen will clear and the following prompt will be displayed on the screen:

Enter Customer Number:

If the customer record number has been found dBASE will display:

The Customer Record has been DELETED

and then control will be returned to the Customer Maintenance Menu.

If a Customer Record Number has not been found, control will be returned to the Customer Maintenance Menu.

SECTION 37
Customer maintenance menu

The program to delete the Customer Record is DELCUST.PRG, type the following at the dot prompt:

.MODIFY COMMAND DELCUST

Press the RETURN key, and type in the listing in Figure 37–6.

Then enter the program to find the Customer Record Number.

At the dot prompt type:

.MODIFY COMMAND CUSTFIND

Press the RETURN key, and type in the listing in Figure 37–7.

```
*********************** DELCUST.PRG ***********************
SET TALK OFF
SET ECHO OFF
     * Find the customer by his customer number
DO CUSTFIND
IF .NOT. FOUNDCUST
     * The customer record has not been found
RETURN
ELSE
     * Delete the customer record
DELETE
PACK
@11,8 SAY "   The Customer Record has been DELETED"
RETURN
ENDIF
RETURN
```

Figure 37–6 The Delete Customer Program

```
*********************** CUSTFIND.PRG ***********************
PUBLIC FOUNDCUST
SET TALK OFF
SET ECHO OFF
FOUNDCUST=.T.
    CLEAR
    ?
    ?
    ?
    ACCEPT " Enter Customer Number: " TO CUSTNO
         * Find the customer record
    LOCATE FOR CUSTNUMBER=CUSTNO
    IF EOF()
         * No such customer record number
    FOUNDCUST=.F.

    RETURN
ENDIF
RETURN
```

Figure 37–7 The Customer Record Number Search Program

183

■ SECTION 37
Customer maintenance menu

If the number three key is pressed when the Customer Maintenance Menu is displayed, option 3 will be selected.

This option will enable you to edit a Customer Record from the existing customer records. Before it is possible to edit a customer record it must be found first, therefore at this point we use our existing program – CUSTFIND.PRG – to find our customer number.

When option three is selected the screen will clear and the following prompt will be displayed on the screen:

Enter Customer Number:

If the customer record number has been found dBASE will then display the customer format screen as used for adding a record, but with the customer details showing, these can now be amended and then saved. Figure 37–8 shows a format screen with the customer record details filled in.

```
Customer Number  :  A002
Cusomer Name     :  LUBRICAL LTD
Address          :  ELTHAM WORKS
                    PRODHOE
                    NORTHUMBERLAND
Postcode         :  NE48 9JP
Discount         :  7.5#
Telephone Number:   0721 433346
Contact Name     :  MARTIN PETERS
```

READ |<B;>|CUSTOMER |Rec: 1/11 |Caps

Figure 37–8

184

■ SECTION 37
Customer maintenance menu

If a Customer Record Number has not been found, control will be returned to the Customer Maintenance Menu.

The program to edit the Customer Records is EDITCUST.PRG, to enter it type the following command at the dot prompt:

.MODIFY COMMAND EDITCUST

Press the RETURN key, and type in the listing in Figure 37–9.

```
********************** EDITCUST.PRG **********************
SET TALK OFF
SET ECHO OFF
    * Find the customer by the customer record number
DO CUSTFIND
IF .NOT. FOUNDCUST
    * No such customer record number
RETURN
ENDIF
    * Use custom format CUSTOMER.FMT
SET FORMAT TO CUSTOMER.FMT
READ
RETURN
```

Figure 37–9 The Edit Customer Record Program

If we returned to the MAIN MENU and selected option number two from the menu, control would then be passed to the Stock Maintenance Menu. This is shown below in Figure 38–1.

■ SECTION 38
Stock maintenance menu

```
++++++++++++++++++++++++++++++++++
+++++ STOCK MAINTENANCE MENU +++++
++++++++++++++++++++++++++++++++++
Option No.         Option
1                  ADD a stock record
2                  DELETE a stock record
3                  EDIT an existing stock record
4                  QUIT return to main menu
     Enter Option Number :
```

```
Command       |<B:>|CUSTOMER        |Rec: 1/11      |         | Caps
```

Figure 38-1

This submenu shows that we are able to perform various tasks with our customer records, these are:

Add a new stock record.

Delete an existing stock record.

Edit an existing stock record.

Quit this menu and return to the main menu.

The program to display this menu is shown in Figure 38-2, and can be typed in from the dot prompt as below:

.MODIFY COMMAND EDPART

■ SECTION 38
Stock maintenance menu

Press the RETURN key and enter the listing in Figure 38-2 below.

```
*********************** EDPART.PRG *******************
SET TALK OFF
SET ECHO OFF
STORE " " TO CHOICE
DO WHILE .T.
    CLEAR
    ?
    ?"             ++++++++++++++++++++++++++++++++++"
    ?"             ++++ STOCK MAINTENANCE MENU ++++"
    ?"             ++++++++++++++++++++++++++++++++++"
    ?
    ?"             Option No.        Option"
    ?
    ?"             1                 ADD a stock record"
    ?
    ?"             2                 DELETE a stock record"
    ?
    ?"             3                 EDIT an existing stock record"
    ?
    ?"             4                 QUIT return to main menu"
    ?
    WAIT"         Enter Option Number : " TO CHOICE
    DO CASE
      CASE CHOICE = "1"
         DO ADDPART
      CASE CHOICE = "2"
         DO DELPART
      CASE CHOICE = "3"
         DO EDITPART
      CASE CHOICE ="4"
         RETURN
    ENDCASE
ENDDO
RETURN
```

Figure 38-2 The Stock Maintenance Program

■ SECTION 38
Stock maintenance menu

If '1' was pressed again to select option two the screen would look as displayed in Figure 38-3.

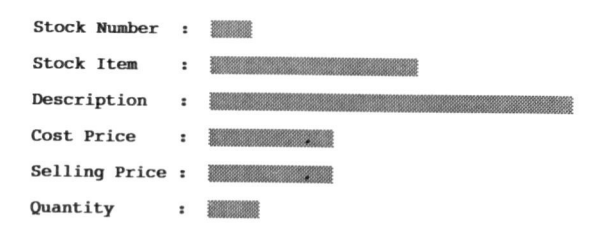

```
Stock Number   :
Stock Item     :
Description    :
Cost Price     :
Selling Price  :
Quantity       :
```

Figure 38-3

To type this program enter at the dot prompt:

.MODIFY COMMAND ADDPART

Press the RETURN key and enter the following:

```
***************** ADDPART.PRG ********************
SET TALK OFF
SET ECHO OFF
USE STOCKFILE
     * Use custom format STOCKFILE.FMT
SET FORMAT TO STOCKFILE.FMT
    APPEND BLANK
    READ
RETURN
```

Figure 38-4 The Adding a Stock Record Program

This program uses the command:

USE STOCKFIL

Stockfil is the database file which must be CREATED before the mainmenu program is run. The details of the file STOCKFIL.dbf are as follows:

SECTION 38
Stock maintenance menu

```
Structure for database: B:STOCKFIL.dbf
Number of data records:      4
Date of last update    : 04/03/88
Field  Field name_  Type          Width      Dec
    1  PART       _ Character       20
    2  PART_NO      Character        4
    3  ITEM       _ Character       35
    4  C_PRICE      Numeric         12         2
    5  S_PRICE      Numeric         12         2
    6  QUANT_       Numeric          5
** Total **                         89
```

To do this from the dot prompt, type:

. CREATE STOCKFIL

Then press the RETURN key and enter the information shown above.

The program ADDPART also uses the program line:

SET FORMAT TO STOCKFIL.FMT

This line is calling up the program STOCKFIL.FMT, which enables dBASE to display as shown in Figure 38–3.

To enter the program STOCKFIL.FMT enter

.MODIFY COMMAND STOCKFIL.FMT

Press the RETURN key and then type the program as shown in Figure 38–5. It is important to remember when creating a format file to type in the extension '.FMT' after the filename when using the MODIFY COMMAND, because if it is not typed in dBASE will automatically assign the extension '.PRG', making it a program file not a format file.

The program will enter information into the .dbf database STOCKFIL at its next record, by using the command APPEND BLANK in the ADDPART program.

```
******************* STOCKFIL.FMT *******************
@6,10   SAY "   Stock Number  : " GET PART_NO
@8,10   SAY "   Stock Item    : " GET PART
@10,10  SAY "   Description   : " GET ITEM
@12,10  SAY "   Cost Price    : " GET C_PRICE
@14,10  SAY "   Selling Price. " GET S_PRICE
@16,10  SAY "   Quantity      : " GET QUANT
```

Figure 38–5 The Stockfil Format Program

SECTION 38
Stock maintenance menu

If the number two key is pressed when the Stock Maintenance Menu was displayed, option 2 will be selected.

This option will enable you to delete a stock item from the existing stock records. Before it is possible to delete a stock record it must be found first, therefore at this point we need to write two programs, one to delete and the other to find the required stock record.

When option two is selected the screen will clear and the following prompt will be displayed on the screen:

Enter Stock Number:

If the stock number has been found dBASE will display:

Stock Item is DELETED

and then control will be returned to the Customer Maintenance Menu.

If a Stock Record Number has not been found, control will be returned to the Stock Maintenance Menu.

The program to delete the Customer Record is DELPART.PRG, type the following at the dot prompt:

.MODIFY COMMAND DELPART

Press the RETURN key, and type in the listing in Figure 38–6.

As with the DELCUST.PRG, which needed the program CUSTFIND.PRG to search for the customer record. The program DELPART.PRG requires a program to search for the Stock number.

At the dot prompt type:

.MODIFY COMMAND STOCKFIN

Press the RETURN key, and type in the listing in Figure 38–7.

SECTION 38
Stock maintenance menu

```
****************** DELPART.PRG ********************
SET TALK OFF
SET ECHO OFF
     * Find Stock Item by Stock Number
DO STOCKFIND
IF .NOT. FOUNDSTK
     * No such Stock Number
RETURN
     ELSE
     * Delete the stock item
DELETE
     PACK
     @11,8 SAY "            Stock Item is DELETED"
RETURN
     ENDIF
RETURN
```

Figure 38–6 The Delete a Stock Item Program

```
****************** STOCKFIND.PRG ******************
PUBLIC FOUNDSTK
SET TALK OFF
SET ECHO OFF
FOUNDSTK=.T.
     CLEAR
     ?
     ?
     ?
     ?
     ?
ACCEPT "           Enter Stock Number: " TO STK_NO
USE STOCKFIL
     LOCATE FOR PART_NO=STK_NO
IF EOF()
     * No such stock number
     FOUNDSTK=.F.
     RETURN
ENDIF
RETURN
```

Figure 38–7 The Stock Number Search Program

If the number three key is pressed when the Stock Maintenance Menu is displayed, option 3 will be selected.

This option will enable you to edit a Stock Record from the existing stock records. Before it is possible to edit a stock record it must be found first, therefore at this point we use our existing program – STOCKFIN.PRG – to find our stock record.

When option three is selected the screen will clear and the following prompt will be displayed on the screen:

Enter Stock Number:

SECTION 38
Stock maintenance menu

If the stock record number has been found dBASE will then display the customer format screen as used for adding a record, but with the stock information showing, these can now be amended and then saved. Figure 38–8 shows a format screen with the stock record information filled in.

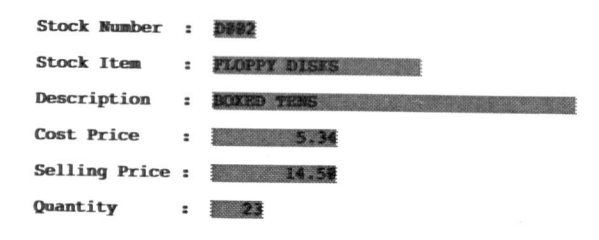

```
Stock Number   : D##2
Stock Item     : FLOPPY DISKS
Description    : BOXED TENS
Cost Price     :         5.34
Selling Price  :        14.5#
Quantity       :    23
```

READ   <B:>STOCKFIL   Rec: 7/26   Caps

Figure 38–8

If a Stock Record Number has not been found, control will be returned to the Stock Maintenance Menu.

The program to edit the Customer Records is EDITPART.PRG, to enter it type the following command at the dot prompt:

.MODIFY COMMAND EDITPART

Press the RETURN key, and type in the listing in Figure 38–9.

```
****************** EDITPART.PRG ******************
SET TALK OFF
SET ECHO OFF
    * Find the Stock Item by the Stock Number
DO STOCKFIND
IF .NOT. FOUNDSTK
    * No such Stock Number
    RETURN
ENDIF
    * Use custom format STOCKFILE.FMT
SET FORMAT TO STOCKFILE.FMT
    READ
RETURN
```

Figure 38–9 The Stock Editing Program

■ SECTION 39
Print menu

So far the programs that we have written only enabled us to view the information on the screen. To complete this small example we will now look at the third option on the main menu – Print Menu.

This option when taken will display a further menu, the Print Menu, the screen will look as in Figure 39–1 below.

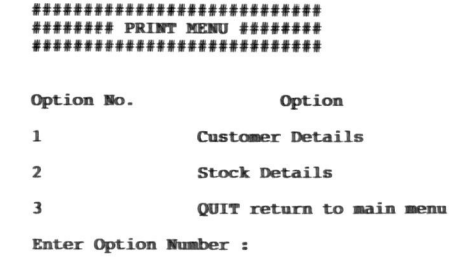

```
#############################
####### PRINT MENU #######
#############################

Option No.              Option
1                       Customer Details
2                       Stock Details
3                       QUIT return to main menu
Enter Option Number :
```

```
Command       |<B:>|STOCKFIL        |Rec: 7/26           |         | Caps
```

Figure 39-1

This submenu shows that we are able to perform various tasks with our customer records, these are:

> **Print Customer Details.**
>
> **Print Stock Details.**
>
> **Exit and Return to Main Menu.**

The program to display the Print Menu is called PRMENU.PRG.

Type at the dot prompt:

> **.MODIFY COMMAND PRMENU**

193

SECTION 39
Print menu

Press RETURN and then enter the listing below in Figure 39–2.

```
****************** PRMENU.PRG *********************
SET TALK OFF
SET ECHO OFF
STORE " " TO CHOICE
DO WHILE .T.
    CLEAR
    ?"                  ############################"
    ?"                  ########  PRINT MENU #######"
    ?"                  ############################"
    ?
    ?
    ?"                  Option No.            Option"
    ?
    ?"                      1             Customer Details"
    ?
    ?"                      2             Stock Details"
    ?
    ?"                      3             QUIT return to main menu"
    ?
    WAIT "             Enter Option Number : " TO CHOICE
    DO CASE
        CASE CHOICE = "1"
            DO CUSTPRN
        CASE CHOICE = "2"
            DO STKPRN
        CASE CHOICE = "3"
            RETURN
    ENDCASE
ENDDO
```

Figure 39–2 The Print Menu Program

If '1' was pressed to select option one the screen would look as displayed in Figure 39–3.

```
    Choose an Option No. to search for customer details :

            Option No.          Option

                1           BY Customer Number

                2           BY Discount Level

                3           QUIT return to main menu

            Enter Option Number :
```

Figure 39–3

■ SECTION 39
Print menu

On this screen the program asks whether one of the following options are wanted:

To search for the required record by Customer Number.

To search for the required record by Discount Level.

To quit and return to the main menu.

If option '1' was selected, the program would then ask you for a Customer Number as shown below in Figure 39–4. This part of the program then uses the database file CUSTOMER.DBF to carry out its search for the Customer Number.

When this has been carried out the Customer Records that have been requested will be printed out, these would look as shown in Figure 39–5.

```
Enter - Start Customer Number ----- AQ001
Enter - End Customer Number -------
```

```
Command        <B:>STOCKFIL          Rec: 7/26                    Caps
```

Figure 39–4

```
Customer Number  : C009
Customer Name    : SCRIBE SYSTEMS
Address          : OLD MILL LANE
                   RIVER WAY
                   OXFORD
Postcode         : OX4 9BY
Discount         : 4 0
Telephone Number : 0863 348756
```

Figure 39–5

195

SECTION 39
Print menu

If option '2' was selected, the program would then ask you for the Discount Level as shown below in Figure 39–6.

When the search has been carried out the Customer Records that have been requested will be printed out, these would look as shown in Figure 39–5.

```
Enter - Lower Discount level ----- 4.0
Enter - Higher Discount level ----
```

```
Command         |<B:>|STOCKFIL              |Rec: 7/25                    | Caps
```

Figure 39–6

The program to carry out the searches and print out the results is shown below in Figure 39–7. To enter the program CUSTPRN.PRG, Type at the dot prompt:

.MODIFY COMMAND CUSTPRN

Press RETURN and enter the listing.

```
****************** CUSTPRN.PRG ********************
SET TALK OFF
SET ECHO OFF
CLEAR
@5,1 SAY " "
?" Choose an Option No. to search for customer details:"
    ?
    ?"                    Option No.            Option"
    ?
    ?"                        1                 BY Customer Number"
    ?
    ?"                        2                 BY Discount Level"
    ?
    ?"                        3                 QUIT return to main menu"
    ?
WAIT "                       Enter Option Number: " TO CHOICE
```

196

■ SECTION 39
Print menu

```
DO CASE
    CASE CHOICE = "1"
    CLEAR
@4,12 SAY " "
    ACCEPT "          Enter — Start Customer Number ——— " TO
SCODE
    ?
    ACCEPT "          Enter — End Customer Number ——— " TO
ECODE
@12,12 SAY "          Customer Numbers must be existing numbers"
@20,1 SAY " Ensure printer is turned on — strike any key to
print"
        USE CUSTOMER
          INDEX ON CUSTNUMBER TO KEYCODE
      SEEK SCODE
SET PRINT ON
    DO WHILE CUSTNUMBER >= SCODE .AND. CUSTNUMBER <= ECODE
? SPACE(12) "Customer Number : " + CUSTNUMBER
? SPACE(12) "Customer Name   : " + CLIENTNAME
? SPACE(12) "Address         : " + ADD1
? SPACE(12) "                 " + ADD2
? SPACE(12) "                 " + ADD3
? SPACE(12) "Postcode        : " + POST-CODE
? SPACE(12) "Discount        : " + STR(DISC,6,2)
? SPACE(12) "Telephone Number: " + TEL_NO
?
?
    SKIP
        ENDDO
CASE CHOICE = "2"
    CLEAR
    @4,12 SAY " "
    ACCEPT "          Enter — Lower Discount level  ——— " TO LCODE
    ?
    ACCEPT "          Enter — Higher Discount level ——— " TO HCODE
@12,12 SAY "          Discount level must be an existing one"
@20,1 SAY " Ensure printer is turned on — strike any key to
print"
        USE CUSTOMER
          INDEX ON DISC TO KEYCODE
      SEEK LCODE
SET PRINT ON
    DO WHILE DISC >= LCODE .AND. DISC <= HCODE
? SPACE(12) "Customer Number : " + CUSTNUMBER
? SPACE(12) "Customer Name   : " + CLIENTNAME
? SPACE(12) "Address         : " + ADD1
? SPACE(12) "                 " + ADD2
? SPACE(12) "                 " + ADD3
? SPACE(12) "Postcode        : " + POST-CODE
? SPACE(12) "Discount        : " + STR(DISC,6,2)
? SPACE(12) "Telephone Number: " + TEL_NO
?
?
    SKIP
        ENDDO
CASE CHOICE = "3"
    RETURN
        ENDCASE
SET PRINT OFF
    CLOSE INDEX
        ERASE KEYCODE.NDX
RETURN
```

Figure 39–7 The Customer Record Print Program

SECTION 39
Print menu

If option '2' was selected from the Print Menu the screen would look as follows:

```
Choose an Option No. to search for stock details
            Option No.         Option
            1                  BY Stock Number
            2                  BY Cost Price
            3                  BY Selling Price
            4                  QUIT return to main menu
            Enter Option Number :
```

| Command | **<B:>**CUSTOMER | Rec: 3/11 | | Caps |

Figure 39–8

This screen asks whether one of the following options are wanted:

To search for the required record by Stock Number.

To search for the required record by Cost Price.

To search for the required record by Selling price.

To quit and return to the main menu.

If option '1' was selected, the program would then ask you for a Stock Number as shown below in Figure 39–9. This part of the program then uses the database file CUSTOMER.DBF to carry out its search for the Stock Number.

SECTION 39
Print menu

When this has been carried out the Stock Records that have been requested will be printed out, these would look as shown in Figure 39–10.

```
Enter - Start Stock Number ------ D001
Enter - End Stock Number --------
```

```
Command          <B:> CUSTOMER              Rec: 3/11                    Caps
```

Figure 39–9

```
Stock Number  : S001
Stock Item    : 5.25 FLOPPY DISKS
Description   : BOXED IN TENS
Cost Price    : 4.39
Selling Price : 8.50
Discount      : 5.0
```

Figure 39–10

SECTION 39

Print menu

If option '2' was selected, the program would then ask you for the Cost Price as shown below in Figure 39–11.

When this has been carried out the Stock Records that have been requested will be printed out, these would look as shown in Figure 39–10.

```
Enter - Lowest Cost price -------- 4.26

Enter - Highest Cost price -------




Command       |<B:>|STOCKFIL               |Rec: 1/26        |       |   Caps
```

Figure 39–11

■ SECTION 39
Print menu

If option '3' was selected, the program would then ask you for the Selling Price as shown below in Figure 39–12.

When this has been carried out the Stock Records that have been requested will be printed out, these would look as shown in Figure 39–10.

The program to carry out the searches and print out the results is shown below in Figure 39–12. To enter the program CUSTPRN.PRG, Type at the dot prompt:

.MODIFY COMMAND STKPRN

Press RETURN and enter the listing below in Figure 39–12.

```
******************* STKPRN.PRG **********************
SET TALK OFF
SET ECHO OFF
    CLEAR
@5,1 SAY " "
    ?" Choose an Option No. to search for stock details"
    ?
    ?"                         Option No.             Option"
    ?
    ?"                             1                  BY Stock Number"
    ?
    ?"                             2                  BY Cost Price"
    ?
    ?"                             3                  BY Selling Price"
    ?
    ?"                             4                  QUIT return to main menu"
    ?
WAIT "                        Enter Option Number : " TO CHOICE
    DO CASE
        CASE CHOICE = "1"
CLEAR
    @5,10 SAY " "
ACCEPT "            Enter - Start Stock Number ———— " TO SCODE
?
ACCEPT "            Enter - End Stock Number ———— " TO ECODE
@ 15,10 SAY " Stock Number must be an existing number"
@ 20,1 SAY " "
WAIT " Ensure Printer is turned on - press any key to print"
        USE STOCKFIL
        INDEX ON PART NO TO KEYCODE
    SEEK SCODE
SET PRINT ON
        DO WHILE PART NO >- SCODE .AND. PART_NO <= ECODE
? SPACE(12) "Stock Number : "+PART_NO
? SPACE(12) "Stock Item   : "+PART
? SPACE(12) "Description  : "+ITEM
? SPACE(12) "Cost Price   : "+ STR(C_PRICE,12,2)
? SPACE(12) "Selling Price: "+ STR(S_PRICE,12,2)
? SPACE(12) "Discount     : "+ STR(QUANT,5)
?
?
```

SECTION 39
Print menu

```
        SKIP
ENDDO
            CASE CHOICE = "2"
CLEAR
@5,10 " " SAY
ACCEPT "                    Enter — Lowest Cost price ─────── " TO LCODE
?
ACCEPT "                    Enter — Highest Cost price ─────── " TO HCODE
@15,10 SAY " Cost price must be an existing Cost price"
@20,1 SAY " "
WAIT " Ensure the printer is turned on — press any key to print"
            USE STOCKFIL
            INDEX ON C_PRICE TO KEYCODE
            SET PRINT ON
         DO WHILE C_PRICE >= LCODE .AND. C_PRICE <= HCODE
? SPACE(12) "Stock Number  : " +PART_NO
? SPACE(12) "Stock Item    : " +PART
? SPACE(12) "Description   : " +ITEM
? SPACE(12) "Cost Price    : " + STR(C_PRICE,12,2)
? SPACE(12) "Selling Price: " + STR(S_PRICE,12,2)
? SPACE(12) "Quantity      : " + STR(QUANT,5)
?
?
            SKIP
       ENDDO
CASE CHOICE = "3"
CLEAR
@5,10 SAY " "
ACCEPT "                    Enter — Lowest Selling price ─────── " TO LCODE
?
ACCEPT "                    Enter — Highest Selling price ─────── " TO HCODE
@15,10 SAY " Selling price must be an existing Selling price"
@20,1 SAY " "
WAIT " Ensure the printer is turned on — press any key to print"
            USE STOCKFIL
            INDEX ON S_PRICE TO KEYCODE
      SEEK LCODE
SET PRINT ON
         DO WHILE S_PRICE >= LCODE .AND. S_PRICE <= HCODE
? SPACE(12) "Stock Number  : " +PART_NO
? SPACE(12) "Stock Item    : " +PART
? SPACE(12) "Description   : " +ITEM
? SPACE(12) "Cost Price    : " + STR(C_PRICE,12,2)
? SPACE(12) "Selling Price: " + STR(S_PRICE,12,2)
? SPACE(12) "Quantity      : " + STR(QUANT,5)
?
?
            SKIP
      ENDDO
CASE CHOICE = "4"
      RETURN
ENDCASE
      SET PRINT OFF
CLOSE INDEX
            ERASE KEYCODE.NDX
RETURN
```

Figure 39–12 The Stock Record print Program

■ SECTION 39
Print menu

This has only been a brief introduction into programming with dBASE. The possibilities even with these small programs is endless, the menu system can be extended to produce invoices, statements, quotations, sales records and even accounts records.

Practise writing small programs like the ones that have been shown in this section, alter them to suit your own needs, even extend them using some of the ideas above.

Index

Add a customer record program, 180
Add a stock record program, 188
APPEND, 60, 64
ASSISTANT, 24
Average, 97

Blackboard, 52
Blackboard editing keys, 53
Bottom of a record, 79
BROWSE, 66
Browse menu, 67

Character field, 14
Columns menu – Report, 114
Conditional statement, 47
Connect, 103
Constant/Expression, 103
COPY, 16, 86
COUNT, 97
CREATE, 34
Ctrl-KW, 59
Customer File, 34
Customer Format program, 182
Customer Maintenance program, 179
Customer Record Print program, 197
Customer Record Search program, 183

Data Entry Form, 50, 55
Database Management System, 10
Date Field, 14
dBASEIII Commands, 162
dBASEIII PLUS Commands, 173
Delete Customer program, 183
Delete Stock program, 191
Diskcopy, 15
DISPLAY, 45
DISPLAY ALL, 146

Display – Labels, 142
          Reports, 128
          Status, 152
DO, 62
Dot prompt, 30, 146

EDIT, 60, 69
Edit Customer Record program, 185
End, 106
Entry of Data, 41
Exit Menu – Query, 108
          Report, 114

Field Description, 37
File types, 13
FORMAT file, 14
Function keys, 153
Function value, 61

GET Command, 58
GO, 79
GOTO, 74
Graphics – Data Entry Form, 55
Group Heading – Report, 118
Groups Menu – Report, 114

Help, 31

Index files, 14
Index key expression, 80
INDEX ON, 150

Labels, 134
Label Contents, 136
Label Size, 138
Left margin, 121
LIST Command, 32, 44
LIST ALL, 146
LOCATE Command, 74
LOCATE FOR, 149
Locate Menu – Report, 114

205

Index

Main Menu program, 177
Memo field, 14
Menu Options, 26
MODIFY Command, 58
Modify Database, 65
Modify Label, 141
Modify Menu, 61
Modify Report, 124
Modify Structure, 91

Operator, 102
Options Menu − Labels, 135
                Report, 113
Organize Menu, 80
Owed file, 92

PACK, 71
Page Title − Report, 117
Page width, 121
Percent file, 82
Position Menu, 77
Print Menu Program, 194
Print Screen, 62
Printing Labels, 143
Printing Reports, 129

Query, 100
Query1 file, 101
Query Menu Bar, 101

READ Command, 58
Record Size, 11

Report, 112
RETRIEVE, 26

Saving a file, 43
SAY Command, 58
Scope submenu, 47
Screen Painter, 50
Set, 154
SET DRIVE, 38
SET FORMAT TO, 60
Set Menu, 158
SET MENU ON/OFF, 147
SET PRINT ON/OFF, 62
Set Up, 28
SKIP, 75
SORT, 92
SORT TO, 151
Start, 106
Stock Editing Program, 192
Stock Format Program, 189
Stock Maintenance Program, 187
Stock Number Search Program, 191
Stock Record Print Program, 201
SUM, 98

Trim Function, 140
TOP of a record, 79

Update Menu, 69
USE, 59